Alan Noble Simpson

Architect.

Edinburgh 1981.

SCOTLAND AND THE UNION

The Novel and the Modern World
Robert Louis Stevenson
Robert Burns
Critical Approaches to Literature
Two Worlds
A Critical History of English Literature
The Paradox of Scottish Culture
Scotch Whisky, its Past and Present
Sir Walter Scott and His World
Robert Burns and His World
Robert Louis Stevenson and His World
James Boswell and His World
Was: a Pastime from Time Past
Charles Edward Stuart: the Life and Times
of Bonnie Prince Charlie

'Riding the Parliament' at the opening of the 1685
Scottish Parliament in the reign of James VII and II.

SCOTLAND
and the
UNION

David Daiches

JOHN MURRAY

Printed and bound in Great Britain by
Butler & Tanner Ltd,
Frome and London
0 7195 3391 0

Contents

Preface

A full explanation of how the Union of Scotland and England
came about in 1707 would require a full history of Scotland up
to that date, while a full account of the consequences of the Union
would require an equally complete account of Scottish history—
social, cultural, economic, political—since 1707. Such a com-
prehensive aim is beyond the scope of this book. What I have
tried to do is to present in as vivid detail as I can the immediate
factors involved in the passing of the Treaty of Union and the
passionate debate about the Union that went on in Scotland in
the years before its enactment. That is the central part of the book,
but I have flanked it with a preceding and succeeding section,
each written on a very much smaller historical scale. The preceding part is a re-telling of Scottish history from the beginnings
up to the Revolution of 1689 in such a way as to pick out those
elements that helped to create and define the Scottish nation and
Scotland's sense of nationhood. The succeeding part, highly
selective and even impressionist, is a presentation of aspects of
Scottish history after the Union in such a way as to illustrate and
draw attention to what seem to me the most important consequences of the Union. In this part of the book, in the space
available to me, I can only provide suggestions and examples
rather than give a continuous history.

I have told the story always from the point of view of Scotland,
which means that I have gone into considerably greater detail
in explaining Scottish motives than in providing equivalent in-
formation about England. I have not attempted, for example, to

give a full account of politics in England in the reign of Queen Anne but present the picture as seen from Edinburgh.

In the central part of the book I have drawn almost entirely on contemporary sources—diaries, letters, speeches, pamphlets, official parliamentary minutes, Acts of Parliament—as my aim has been to give the reader a sense of immediate involvement in the debates and controversies. I have quoted these sources in the original spelling, because this seems to me to add to their period flavour and so help the reader to project himself into the historical situation. Some of my preparation was done in the National Library of Scotland, whose staff I found consistently courteous and helpful. But the bulk of it was done in my own study with the help of my own library of Scottish books that I have been building up for some forty years and which contains a large number of books and pamphlets of the early eighteenth century. I mention this to emphasize that this book is a product of a long period of reflection on Scottish history and culture, illustrated in the build-up of my own library, rather than a work hastily compiled in response to the present interest in Scottish devolution.

At the same time, this book *is* a response to that interest, and I hope that it will help to provide depth and perspective to arguments put forward both by Scottish Nationalists and their opponents. As the following pages will show, most of those arguments are very much older than many people realize.

D. D.

1. Scotland Emerges

The 'incorporating union' of Scotland and England that took place in 1707, after bitter debates in the Scottish Parliament, which was abolished by the Act of Union, was a union of a smaller and poorer country with a larger and richer one. The relations between the two countries had been through many phases before this merger was effected, and before we can begin to understand the nature of these relations and the feelings of Scotsmen about a union with England we must ask some elementary questions about the identity of the smaller partner. In what sense was Scotland a separate 'country' before 1707? What was Scottish nationhood and how did it come into being? How did the Scots come to be differentiated as such and in what sense were the inhabitants of Lowland Scotland different in origins, language and culture from those of northern England? Though these questions are elementary, they are not simple, for the development of the Scottish nation was a highly complex affair, and there was a flourishing Kingdom of Scotland long before there could be said to have been any real sense of Scottish national identity. We must go back into history if we want to understand what was involved.

When Agricola advanced northward in A.D. 80 to seek a northern frontier for the Roman province of Britannia he found in the Lowlands of Scotland Celtic Britons similar to those the Romans had found in England, while in the more northerly parts (which the Romans called 'Caledonia' after the name of one of the tribes there) there were the people known as the Picts. The Picts, like the Lowland tribes, though culturally quite separate from them, were largely a Celtic people, and spoke a variety of the branch of the Celtic languages known as P-Celtic. The Lowland tribes spoke another variety of P-Celtic. The latter came under intermittent Roman domination and were in some degree Romanised: the Picts or *Caledonii* remained a constant threat to Roman Britain from the north in spite of a number of Roman expeditions into their country. When the Romans had to withdraw from Britain because of pressure on the Roman Empire elsewhere, they left the Romanized Britons to face alone the attacks of Angles, Saxons and Jutes from northern Germany and Denmark in the fifth and sixth centuries. There was still no Scottish people and the area that became Scotland was inhabited by a variety of tribes, of whom the most widely settled were the Picts north of the Forth–Clyde line.

The Scots were a Gaelic-speaking (Q-Celtic) people settled in northern Ireland, and about the year 500 a member of their royal house called Fergus Mór led a colony of Scots from Ireland to settle in the west of Scotland where they established the kingdom of Dalriada. It was this settlement of Fergus that was to determine that the country would eventually be called Scotland, and it is from him that all subsequent kings and queens of Scotland and eventually Great Britain are descended. So in the sixth century there were both Picts and Scots to the north and west of the Forth–Clyde line, while between that line and the Tyne–Solway line were British tribes who coalesced to produce a number of fairly substantial kingdoms, including Strathclyde in the west and south-west, Gododdin in the east, and Rheged, immediately north and south of the Solway. These kingdoms came under threat from the kingdom the Angles had established in Northumbria, and in the seventh century we find the Northumbrian Angles in control of much of southern Scotland outside Strathclyde. There they imposed their culture and introduced the Anglian, northern form of English, which in Scotland was to develop into Scots.

Britons of Strathclyde, Scots (both now Christian) and Picts (still largely pagan) warred against each other, but the threat posed by invading Norsemen helped to bring them together.

(It was not until 1266 that the western isles were returned by the Norse to the Scottish crown, while Orkney and Shetland were not acquired until 1468-9.) Then about 843, perhaps as a result of a valid claim through marriage, perhaps by conquest, perhaps by both these means, the Scottish king of Dalriada, Kenneth MacAlpin, acquired the throne of the Picts and united Dalriada and Pictland under his own rule. And so the kingdom of Scotland was born, *Alba* in Gaelic, *Scotia* in Latin, and the Picts with their language and their culture disappear from history, leaving as their chief visible monument their intriguing symbol stones. The MacAlpin kings continued to rule in what was now Scotland, and turned their attention eastward and southward to Northumbrian-controlled Lowland Scotland. They captured Edinburgh late in the tenth century and by 1043, under King Duncan, Scotland's boundaries were pretty much as we know them today.

Scottish kings never succeeded for long in asserting their rule further south, though they tried. Duncan's son, Malcolm III, would have liked to extend his kingdom southward to the Tees, but the Normans now ruled England and Scottish soldiers were no match for Norman knights. William Rufus came north in 1092 to push back the expanding Scots and the line from Solway to Tweed was now fixed permanently as his northern and Scotland's southern boundary. The Norman kings of England posed a constant threat to the independence of the Scottish kingdom. In 1072 William the Conqueror came north to the old Pictish centre of Abernethy on the Tay, where Malcolm III (Canmore) recognized him as his overlord: this was a recognition of Norman power and influence but it did not affect the existence of Scotland as a separate kingdom under her own king.

The real Norman influence in Scotland came not from concessions of English overlordship but from penetration of Scotland by Norman settlers. The process began, paradoxically enough, when Malcolm Canmore's English wife Margaret, considering the Scots to be barbarians, encouraged the importation of Normans and Norman ideas to help run both church and state. The paradox lies in the fact that Margaret was the sister of

Edward Atheling ('the heir'), the representative of the old Saxon line ousted by William the Conqueror in 1066, and had been brought up in Hungary. So the first significant wave of Norman or Anglo-French influence in Scotland was begun by a Saxon-Hungarian Scottish queen. Throughout the twelfth century Anglo-Norman, Anglo-Breton and Anglo-Flemish barons and knights were encouraged to settle in Scotland by the grant of lands in exchange for military service. They were especially encouraged by David I (1124–53). They brought a structured feudalism to Lowland Scotland; they brought their skills as managers and civil servants that gave new life and energy to the functioning of the ancient Scottish kingship; they strengthened the organization of the church and brought it into touch with continental currents of thought; they built their 'motte-and-bailey' castles; and, when the final crunch came, they organized and led Scottish national resistance to English attempts at conquest. Some of the greatest names in Scottish history are originally Norman. Robert the Bruce was descended from an Anglo-French family that had originally lived in Brix (hence Bruce) in western Normandy and came over to England with William the Conqueror. William Wallace was descended from Richard Wallace, *Walensis*, 'the Welshman', who came to Ayrshire from the Welsh border in Shropshire. Walter the Steward, whose marriage to Margery Bruce founded the royal Stewart dynasty, was descended from a Breton family, his ancestors having held the office of *dapifer* or steward to the archbishops of Dol, near Mont St Michael. Professor G. W. S. Barrow has listed some of the characteristically Scottish names that derive from the importation of Normans into Scotland, especially between the years 1153 and 1214, in the reigns of the brothers Malcolm IV and his successor William the Lion, who had a Norman mother. They include Agnew, Hay, Sinclair, Ramsay, Boswell, Menzies (de Mesnieres), Montgomery, Fraser and Grant.

So if during much of the later Middle Ages Scotland was allied with France against her 'auld enemy' England, it was at the same time the Anglo-French element in Scottish society that strength-

ened the Scottish kingdom and enabled it to maintain its independence against England. In spite of all this there was no real chance
that the French language would compete against Scots and Gaelic
for a place as the central Scottish language. Scots who wax sentimental over the 'auld alliance' and cite the handful of French
words that came into Scots mostly in the late sixteenth century
during the reign of Mary Queen of Scots, forget that for long it
was England that was more firmly in the orbit of French culture,
that from 1066 until the middle of the fourteenth century Norman
French was the polite language of England, that throughout much
of the Middle Ages the English crown ruled large tracts of France
and Englishmen moved freely between the two countries and the
two languages. Scotland was never as much involved with
France as that, and certainly in the twelfth and thirteenth centuries,
when the idea of a Scottish kingdom involving a variety of
people with different traditions and different speech slowly gave
way to the idea of a single nation proud of its Scottish nationality,
the linguistic struggle was between the northern form of English
that had developed into what we call Scots, and Gaelic, the
Q-Celtic language of the original Scots. (The mediaeval Scots
called the Scots language 'Inglis' and tended to call Gaelic 'Scottis'
or 'Ersch'.) The Scots language won the struggle in Edinburgh
and the Lowlands generally and Gaelic was steadily pushed to the
north and west though it remained longer in Galloway and
Buchan. Many Lowland Scots, however, were bi-lingual in
Scots and Gaelic in the Middle Ages.

Many Scots barons also held land in England, and since they
did homage to the English king for their English lands their sense
of Scottish national identity hardly existed. Indeed, it was the
practice of Scottish kings doing homage to English kings for the
lands they held in England that gave the English kings an excuse
for seeking complete domination over the kingdom of Scotland.
As for the king of Scotland, he knew he was king of a number of
diverse peoples, even if they were all called Scots in the one
phrase containing the word that was in common use, that desig-
nating the king's own title, King of Scots. In these circumstances

it is remarkable that a sense of nationhood was built up and permeated all social classes. The sequence of events that hastened, if it did not altogether cause this process, began with the death of Alexander III of Scotland in 1286 leaving the throne to his infant granddaughter Margaret, whose father was Eric II of Norway, whom Alexander's daughter had married. The infant Margaret, 'The Maid of Norway', was sent home from Norway to Scotland, but died in Orkney in 1290 on the journey there. The result was a bitterly disputed succession to the Scottish throne, and the invitation to Edward I of England to prevent civil war by acting as arbitrator. An invitation to an outside power to act as arbitrator in an affair of this kind did not in itself carry any implication of that arbitrator's suzerainty. Edward I, however, had his own ideas.

There were thirteen candidates in all, but the two principals were John Balliol and Robert Bruce, who were both descended from William the Lion's younger brother, David Earl of Huntingdon. Balliol was descended from David's elder daughter Margaret and Bruce from his younger daughter Isabella, so in terms of strict primogeniture Balliol had the better claim. But neither the old Scottish nor the old Pictish form of succession was strictly in terms of primogeniture. King Edward chose Balliol, having already used his position as arbitrator to insist that the claimants should recognize his suzerainty over Scotland. Having chosen Balliol, Edward imposed humiliating conditions on him, determined to show that Balliol was a vassal of his and held Scotland under the English king. Balliol was not a strong man, but the Scottish nobility resented on his behalf the humiliations to which Edward subjected him, and when in 1294 Balliol was called to London and ordered to supply men and money for King Edward's wars against France, the Scots formed a council of four bishops, four earls and four barons which formally concluded a treaty of alliance with France against England. They forced Balliol to renounce his homage to Edward. The result was a successful military campaign by Edward in Scotland, his dismissal of Balliol as king, and his imposition of direct English rule on

Scotland. The defeat of the Scots by the English at Dunbar on 27 April 1296 put an end for the time being to the independent kingdom of Scotland. Edward now regarded Scotland as a conquered province, and any resistance to English rule he treated as high treason to be punished with the gruesome savagery such a crime always met with at that time.

Everything now depended on the attitude of the barons of Scotland. They were not in principle wholly opposed to the union of England and Scotland provided that the kingdom of Scotland retained its distinct identity, and in 1290 the 'Guardians' —two earls, two bishops and two barons, 'chosen by the community of the realm'—had agreed to a union of the two kingdoms by marriage provided this condition was fulfilled. The proposal proved abortive, for Edward made demands that were refused in the name of 'the community of the realm of Scotland'. After Edward's imposition of direct rule in 1296 the Guardians, again acting on behalf of 'the whole community of the realm', organized and carried out resistance.

What the Scottish barons precisely meant by their phrase 'the whole community of the realm' is difficult to determine, but it certainly indicates some sort of sense of national unity, at least among their own baronial class in Scotland. When Andrew Moray and William Wallace temporarily liberated Scotland from English occupation in 1297 they did so as leaders of 'the army of the kingdom of Scotland'. Wallace won a victory at Stirling in 1297 but his army was unable to resist the cavalry that Edward brought with him to Scotland in 1298 and Wallace was defeated at Falkirk in that year, betrayed, taken to England, and savagely tortured and executed as a traitor. He had already become a Scottish popular hero, and has remained so to the present day; but the really interesting point is that he clearly secured the support of the Scottish peasantry for whom the question of which distant king ruled their country had no practical implications whatever. Certainly the garrisoning of Scottish castles by Edward's forces, who imposed taxes, extorted levies and called men up for military service, helped to move them into a state of national opposition to English claims of conquest. The Scottish barons, many of whom also owned lands in England, had more of a struggle to define their Scottish identity against the English, though once they did so (and a good number did not) they organized resistance and encouraged national feeling in order to strengthen it. When Robert Bruce (grandson of the original claimant, who had died in 1295, leaving a son who died in 1304) emerged in the early years of the fourteenth century as Wallace's successor in the struggle against England, the idea of national independence (associated with the words 'freedom' and 'nation') was now firmly established among those who fought with him.

Edward was determined to unite England and Scotland under his rule, and the plans he made for governing the united kingdom were in themselves sensible and even imaginative. But they involved treating any opposition from Scotland as treason, and after the exploits of Wallace and his subsequent fate it was too late for Edward to project himself among the Scots as a wise and peace-loving advocate of a civilized union. When Robert Bruce had himself crowned King of Scots at the traditional Scottish coronation centre of Scone on 27 March 1306, it looked as though this could be no more than a barren gesture, for Edward's forces in Scotland were strong and Bruce was continuously hunted and harried. After a series of nearly disastrous failures, the tide slowly began to turn, and the death of Edward I in the course of an advance into Scotland at Burgh-upon-Sands in Cumberland in 1307, leaving his throne to the much weaker Edward II, gave new heart to the Scots. One by one Bruce's forces captured the strongholds that had been held in Scotland by the English, and Bruce successfully turned too against his Scottish enemies (notably John Comyn, Earl of Buchan). Finally, Bruce's army defeated Edward's much larger English army at Bannockburn on 24 June 1314, and the battle was decisive, though the independence of the kingdom of Scotland was not formally recognized by England until Edward III signed the Treaty of Northampton in 1328.

The English tried to use the Papacy to undermine the independence of the Scottish kingdom, but Bruce fought back (he refused to accept papal missives not addressed to him as King of Scots) and, with the authority of the Church in Scotland, made a remarkable approach to Pope John XXII with the famous Declaration of Arbroath, a letter sent to the Pope from the town's famous old abbey and probably written by Bruce's chancellor Bernard de Linton, Abbot of Arbroath. This passionate and eloquent document recited, in sonorous Latin prose, the causes and course of their war of independence against England and the wrongs done against them by the King of England. It continued:

> For so long as but one hundred men of us remain alive, we shall never under any conditions submit to the domination of the English. It is not for glory or riches or honours that we fight, but only for liberty, which no good man will consent to lose but with his life. (*Non enim propter gloriam, divitias aut honores pugnamus sed propter libertatem solummodo . . .*)

This is a remarkable declaration, and with its association of liberty with the independence of the kingdom, difficult to parallel in the Europe of its time. In its introductory paragraph the Declaration of Arbroath refers with pride to the Scottish nation, traces its history 'from Greater Scythia across the Tyrrhenian Sea and beyond the Pillars of Hercules' until eventually 'we came to our abode in the West where we now dwell. The Britons were driven out; the Picts were utterly destroyed; we were assailed again and again by Norse, Angle and Dane: but by many a victory and endless toil we established ourselves here, and . . . we have ever held our land free from servitude of every kind.' This is romantic pseudo-history, and wholly ignores the multiple make-up of the Scottish people, identifying them only with the original Scots who first emigrated to Scotland. The fact that the Abbot who drafted the declaration must himself have been of Norman stock, as was their national hero Bruce, does not seem to have worried anybody. Britons, Picts, Angles and Anglo-Normans as well as descendants of the original Scots were all part of the Scottish people, but it is evidence of the strength of the sense of national identity, that the wars of independence had generated, that the Declaration of Arbroath stressed the historic unity and continuity of Scotsmen as a people as the ultimate justification for their insistence on the political independence of the kingdom. There were of course those in Scotland who had opposed Wallace and Bruce and supported Edward. And there were, and would long remain as an unhappy characteristic of Scottish society, bitter feuds between both Lowland magnates and Highland clans. But at this moment at the end of the second decade of the fourteenth century the various elements that made up the people of Lowland Scotland and the Gaelic-speaking *Gaidhealtachd* of the Highlands shared a common feeling of Scottish identity. It was perhaps significant in this respect that Bruce was also Earl of Carrick in view of his father's marriage to the daughter and heir of the last Celtic Earl of Carrick, and thus also possessed Celtic blood and a Celtic title.

How deep and permanent was the sense of Scottish national identity voiced so eloquently by the Declaration of Arbroath is a difficult question to answer. In a sense it was a short-lived rush of national emotion produced by specific historical circumstances. It was certainly not sustained at this level in subsequent centuries. But the memory of Wallace and Bruce and Bannockburn and the Declaration of Arbroath remained, as something to be drawn on for comfort and inspiration when historical circumstances again made them relevant. The fourteenth-century Scots poet John Barbour wrote a long poem, *The Bruce*, describing the life and adventures of Robert Bruce and his companions. It includes an outburst about freedom (by which he clearly meant the political independence of a kingdom) that has become a classic expression of Scottish emotion:

A! fredome is a noble thing!
Fredome mayss mad to haiff liking, [enables a man to please himself]
Fredome all solace to man giffis:
He lefys at ess that frely lyvys.

'He lives at ease that freely lives.' It was a new concept of the meaning of freedom from political domination by another country. The late fifteenth-century romance telling the story of William Wallace, attributed to Henry the Minstrel or 'Blind Harry', is further removed from history than Barbour's work, but it shows the same passionate Scottish feeling. When an early eighteenth-century modernization of it by Hamilton of Gilbart-field fell into the hands of the young Robert Burns he later reported that 'it poured a Scottish prejudice in my veins which will boil along there till the flood-gates of life shut in eternal rest'.

The national stability that Scotland seemed to have achieved under Bruce proved to be short-lived. Bruce died in 1329 leaving his kingdom to his five-year-old son David, the first of many Scottish kings to succeed as a minor thereby exacerbating the problem of the relationship between the Crown and the powerful Scottish magnates who owned large tracts of the country spanning the Lowlands and the Highlands, 'two cultures of Celtic and Anglo-Saxon speech lying in only partially feudalized relation-ship to the crown', as Rosalind Mitchison has aptly summed the matter up. And always the English kings were there, waiting to take advantage of any Scottish weakness. Alternating periods of Anglo-Scottish warfare and of reluctantly maintained truces became the pattern, with the Scots periodically renewing their 'auld alliance' with France to strengthen them against the common enemy, England. English troops periodically overran southern Scotland but England lacked the resources to occupy it per-manently.

The reigns of the first two Stewart kings who succeeded David II, Robert II (1371–90) and the feeble Robert III (1390–1406) were marked by sporadic Border fighting, which continued through-out the fifteenth century, generally carried out by Border raiders on each side rather than by the royal forces. By the end of the fourteenth century it was clear that for certain Scottish Border families fighting the English on their own account had become an established and not unattractive way of life. But it was difficult to prevent English incursions into Scotland as far as Edinburgh, as anyone who has driven from Otterburn (where the second Earl

Douglas defeated Percy in 1388, though he himself was killed in
the battle) into Scotland over Carter Bar and looked down on
Edinburgh from Soutra Hill will realize. One of Scotland's
problems in her military relations with England was that her
capital was so near to and accessible from the Border, whereas
England's capital was nearly 350 miles away.

In spite of the struggles between the Crown and the Baronage
which went on intermittently throughout the fifteenth century
the prestige of the Crown and its association with a feeling of
pride in the Scottish nation was (except for a few isolated mo-
ments) maintained. The Highlands and Islands presented a different
but related problem. In north-west Scotland and in the Islands the
heads of the powerful Clan Donald had adopted the title of
Lord of the Isles about 1354, installed themselves with ancient
Celtic pomp and ceremony, and acted as heads of an *imperium in
imperio*. It was to the English king's interest to weaken the
Scottish king by encouraging his powerful subjects in rebellion.
In 1411 Henry IV encouraged Donald, second Lord of the Isles,
to assert his claim to the Earldom of Ross, while the Duke
of Albany, then regent, wanted the earldom for his own son.
An invasion by the Lord of the Isles in support of his claim was
stopped before it reached Aberdeen in the bloody battle of Har-
law. This represented clans and magnates fighting among themselves rather than against the King. England was directly involved,
however, in 1462 when Edward IV made an agreement with John,
fourth Lord of the Isles and James, ninth Earl of Douglas (who had
been exiled by James II and his estates forfeited) by which the
Lord of the Isles would divide with one of his kinsmen rule of
Scotland north of the Forth and Douglas would get back his
estates in the south. Edward IV proved to be too insecure to help
implement a scheme that would have destroyed the kingdom of
Scotland, but the fact that there were powerful Scotsmen both in
Gaelic Scotland and in the south of the country who contem-
plated such a break-up indicates something of the problems that
faced the kings of Scotland in the fifteenth century. James IV
exerted himself forcefully both against the robber barons of the

Borders and against the Lord of the Isles, compelling the surrender and forfeiture of John, fourth Lord of the Isles, in 1493–4 and experimenting with new governmental devices and offices to bring the Highlands and Islands firmly under the control of central government. The result was only temporarily successful, for by using some Highland clans (notably the Campbells) as government agents against others, he perpetuated inter-clan animosities that were to bear grim fruit centuries later.

In spite of the frequent minorities and the struggles between the kings and their over-mighty subjects, the late fifteenth and early sixteenth centuries saw Scotland achieve a new kind of cultural confidence. This was the great age of Middle Scots literature, when the Scots language achieved a richness of poetic expression that put it on a par with any in Europe. Music flourished as never before. Universities were established at St Andrews, Glasgow and Aberdeen. Printing was introduced. Parliament was made more efficient both by a clearer definition of those eligible to be summoned to it (theoretically, only tenants-in-chief) and the establishment of a committee to prepare the agenda, that was to develop into the later notorious Lords of the Articles. Institutions for the administration of justice were improved. The burghs grew in importance, and sought a staple port in the Low Countries. More and more as the fifteenth century developed Scotland became a part of emergent Renaissance Europe, and James IV played his part on the European stage as a Renaissance prince. Though he later turned to the support of Scotland's old ally France, which led to his invasion of England in 1513 and his defeat and death in the disastrous battle of Flodden, he had married a daughter of Henry VII of England—which was to give his great-grandson a successful claim to the English throne. James V, once he had got rid of regents and established his own rule, played the part of Renaissance prince with even greater confidence and with positive swagger.

James V died in 1542, in his thirty-first year, broken-hearted at the ignominious defeat of his army by the English at Solway Moss. He left an infant daughter, known to history as Mary Queen of

Scots, whose reign ushered in decades of internal struggle between pro-French and pro-English forces, exacerbated by the religious element that entered politics after Henry VIII of England abandoned the Church of Rome and religious reformers became active in Scotland. With France still Catholic and England Protestant, and young Mary educated in France and married briefly (for he died soon after) to the Dauphin of France, the recipe was for certain civil war, with France and England supporting different sides. What followed—Mary's marriage to Darnley and the birth in 1567 of their son James, Darnley's murder, Mary's imprisonment, escape, defeat in battle and flight to England where she was eventually executed as a threat to Queen Elizabeth—constitutes one of the most dramatic and turbulent phases of Scottish history. Out of it emerged young James VI, first dominated by tutors and fought over by competing magnates, then, still in his teens, emerging as a king with his own ideas and his own strategy. Scotland had been declared officially Protestant by the Parliament of 1560 and James had been educated by Protestant scholars. But he objected equally to extreme Calvinism and to Roman Catholicism, and tried to steer a moderate Protestant course between them.

James VI on the whole was a good and effective king of Scotland, who managed his subjects well and was able to enlist most of the more powerful ones into his service. He was a scholar and a writer, proud of his Latin learning and eager to show off his scholarship in classics and divinity. In political and ecclesiastical policy he walked a tightrope, never losing sight of his immediate aim of managing Scotland effectively and his longer-term aim of being recognized by Queen Elizabeth as her heir, even if this meant tamely accepting Elizabeth's execution of his mother (whom, however, he had never really known, having been separated from her in earliest infancy). His policy succeeded. On Elizabeth's death in March 1603 James VI of Scotland became also James I of England: for the first time, with the acquiescence of both countries, one king legitimately ruled over them both.

James was more successful as King of Scotland before 1603 than

as King of England after 1603, partly because in England he faced
problems with which he was less familiar, partly because he grew
less flexible and perceptive as he grew older. But from the beginning of his reigning in both countries he saw himself as eventually
king of a united Britain. He spoke eloquently on this subject in
a speech in the Upper House of Parliament in 1604:

> Hath not God first vnited these two Kingdomes both in Language,
> Religion, and similitude of maners? Yea, hath hee not made vs all
> in one Island, compassed with one Sea, and of it selfe by nature so
> indiuisible, as almost those that were borderers themselues on the
> late Borders, cannot distinguish, nor know, or discerne their owne
> limits? These two Countries being separated neither by Sea, nor
> great Riuer, Mountaine, nor other strength of nature, but onely by
> little small brookes, or demolished little walles, so as rather they
> were diuided in apprehension, then in effect; And now in the end and
> fulnesse of time vnited, the right and title of both in my Person,
> alike lineally descended of both the Crownes, whereby it is now
> become like a little World within it selfe, being intrenched and
> fortified round about with a naturall, and yet admirable strong
> pond or ditch, whereby all the former feares of this Nation are now
> quite cut off: ... What God hath conioyned then, let no man
> separate. I am the Husband, and all the whole Isle is my lawfull
> Wife; I am the Head, and it is my Body; I am the Shepherd, and it
> is my flocke: I hope therefore no man will be so vnreasonable as to
> thinke that I that am a Christian King vnder the Gospel, should be
> a Polygamist and husband to two wiues; that I being the Head,
> should haue a diuided and monstrous Body; or that being the
> Shepheard to so faire a Flocke (whose fold hath no wall to hedge it
> but the foure Seas) should haue my Flocke parted in two.

He spelled out his aim even more clearly in a speech of 1607:

> I desire a perfect Vnion of Lawes and persons, and such a Naturalizing
> as may make one body of both Kingdomes vnder mee your King,
> That I and my posteritie (if it so please God) may rule ouer you to
> the worldes end; Such an Vnion as was of the Scots and Pictes in
> Scotland, and of the Heparchie here in England. And for Scotland I
> auow such an Vnion, as if you had got it by Conquest, but such a
> Conquest as may be cemented by loue, the onely sure bond of

subiection or friendship: that as there is ouer both but *vnus Rex*, so
there may be in both but *vnus Grex* and *vna Lex:* for no more possible
is it for one King to gouerne two Countreys *Contiguous*, the one a
great, the other a lesse, a richer and a poorer, the greater drawing like
an Adamant the lesser to the Commodities thereof, then for one
head to gouerne two bodies, or one man to be husband of two wiues,
whereof Christ himself said, *Ab initio non fuit sic.*

The similarities between the two countries were not quite as
great as James maintained. Scots was still the spoken language of
Lowland Scotland, and though it was closely akin to English it
had its distinctive grammar, vocabulary and pronunciation.
(James made no reference at all to the Gaelic-speaking Highlands
and Islands.) It is true that as Protestant Scotland turned away
from Catholic France to a Protestant England, English forms more
and more invaded the speech of those Scotsmen who looked to
England: John Knox's *History of the Reformation in Scotland* was
written in a deliberately Anglicised Scots and Scottish Protestants
looked to English versions of the Bible, first the Geneva Bible of
1560 and then the Authorised Version of 1611. Further, the
departure of James from Scotland in 1603 left Scotland without a
royal Court, the only significant source of patronage for the arts
available to a poor country like Scotland, without the tradition
of Great House patronage of the arts found in Tudor and Stewart
England. Scottish Court poets came south with James, to try their
hand at poetry in standard English which for them was an arti-
ficial language learned from books. As Scottish writers looked to
England for a reading public their written language became more
and more that of their English neighbours even though they
generally continued to speak in Scots. The dimensions of the
problem this posed for Scottish culture were not fully discernible
until the eighteenth century.

James's vision was of a unified Britain with a unified culture. It
was a vision he proved unable to realize, for the political, religious
and cultural factors in the two countries were too complicated
to allow a Union of the Crowns to develop effortlessly into that
'incorporating union' of the two countries that English politicians

were later to work for and eventually to achieve for reasons rather different from those that prompted James's dream of union. '*Quae Deus Coniunxit Nemo Separet*' was the motto James inscribed on the post-1603 Scottish crown piece: 'What God has joined let no man separate.' But men on both sides of the Border continued for more than a century to argue bitterly over what exactly was and should be joined and what exactly was and should be separate.

2. One King, Two Countries

James VI and I began his reign as King of both Scotland and England by persuading the Parliaments of both kingdoms to appoint commissioners to consider the possibilities of a more complete union. The English commissioners were empowered to consider 'such a union of the said realmes of England and Scotland . . . convenient and necessary for the honour of His Majestie, and the weale and common good of both the said realmes', while the Scottish commissioners were asked 'to confer, treat, and consulte upoun a perfyte unioun of the realmes of Scotland and England . . . not dirogating ony wayes ony fundamentall lawes, ancient privileges, offices, richtis, dignities, and liberties of this kingdome'. Both Parliaments were suspicious of the proposals, the English even more than the Scots. The English Parliament simply shelved the project, and although the Scottish Parliament passed an Act of Union on 11 August 1607, this was conditional on England's acceptance, so nothing came of it. The English resented the trooping of Scotsmen into England on James's coming there, and regarded Scotland as a poor and barren country that could be of no use to them. And although the Scottish Parliament approved the project for union, there was no real feeling in the country in favour of it in spite of the fact that the only sustained argument in favour of James's scheme that survives is the treatise by one of the Scottish commissioners, Sir Thomas Craig, written largely in 1605. This work, written in Latin under the title *De Unione Regnorum Britanniae Tractatus* ('A Treatise on the Union of the British Realms') remained unpublished until 1909, when Sanford Terry edited it with a translation. Some of its arguments are worth looking at.

The kings of England since the Norman Conquest, Craig argued, had always aimed to unite the two kingdoms, because 'England would never have peace at home nor take her rightful position abroad so long as a hostile neighbour dwelt so near upon her borders'. The 'more warlike and ambitious' English kings tried to achieve a union by conquest, while 'the wiser, holding such a method questionable, and its results wholly unsatisfactory, sought to unite the two dynasties by marriage'. Craig alleged that 'the objections to union urged by our own people, and their criticisms of the recent conference in London, have not been advanced with the object of weakening or impeding the proposed union, but rather to strengthen it and rivet it the more securely. Scotsmen, in fact, are eager to embrace the proposed union and to hand it down to posterity firmly knit and compact.'

Craig went on to 'consider what things are essential to the proposed union, infusion, or engrafting of the two kingdoms'. He argued that 'to bring it to a fitting and real perfection, everything which tends to diversity and distinction must be removed, while everything conducive to the formation of a single society, and the rooting of the one state in the very bowels (as it were) of the other, must be generously encouraged'. The antagonism between Scotsmen and Englishmen was a mindless tradition carried on automatically by successive generations on both sides of the Border. 'So long as two different names [for the two kingdoms] exist, so long, and on the slightest occasion, a recrudescence may be expected; one side being resolved to assert its superiority and the other to suffer no slight. Why, at the present time, children in their mimic battles call themselves English and Scots, implying thereby a resolve to struggle their hardest for the victory of their own side. The English, also, when they teach their children archery, encourage them to take aim by saying, "There's a Scot! shoot him!" and the youngster boasts a Scottish life for every arrow in his quiver.' If both kingdoms were united in the common title of Britain, such animosities would quickly fade. A common British patriotism would unite the whole island against a potential invader and advance the prosperity of the whole country.

With the two kingdoms united in a single realm, Craig argues, the Border country will no longer be a scene of continuous strife, but 'houses and castles will once more teem with inhabitants; woods, pleasure gardens, and vegetable gardens will add to their amenities and the rich harvests of our waters and flocks will be obtained in security'. He dilates on the advantages of perpetual peace within Britain. As for the Scottish objection to the King's being resident in England, he counters that the King's presence is often an expensive luxury and courtiers can prove a nuisance. Further, the King 'may graciously accord us the occasional light of his royal presence to remedy error and injustice', and when he does come north he will have 'a train of English nobles in his suite' out of whom Scottish citizens and tradesmen can expect to make a profit. Complete free trade throughout Britain will benefit both English and Scots.

Two conditions are necessary for a permanent reconciliation and union 'between two proud and spirited peoples . . . The first is, that the agreement must be of a character consonant with the dignity of both nations. In the second place, the status of neither must suffer the slightest diminution.' (This hardly agrees with his earlier argument that under a union England will have all the advantages of a complete conquest of Scotland.) The union should 'place the two kingdoms on an equality of dignity'. Each should maintain its own manners and customs and be governed by its own laws insofar as that is consonant with a general harmonising of the legal framework. And—surprisingly, in view of the form the union of the two countries was eventually to take—each was to retain its own Parliament with its own 'status and authority' and 'the resolutions of one Parliament must not be liable to rejection or amendment, as it is called, by the other'.

Craig's treatise, supported by much recourse to classical authors and to classical and mediaeval history, does not provide a constitution for a united Britain. Many of his arguments are highly theoretical, some are mutually self-contradictory, and when he points to the concrete advantages of union he is not always careful to reconcile the advantages he foresees for one country with the advantages he foresees for the other. He sees no linguistic problem and is oblivious of the cultural problems of Scotland. His views can hardly have been representative of any large number of his countrymen, and they were certainly not shared by the English Parliament. But it is worth noting that at the beginning of the seventeenth century there were more Scotsmen in favour of a complete union of Scotland and England than there were Englishmen. It is one of the many paradoxes of Scottish history that when such a union was eventually achieved, a century later, the situation in this respect was reversed.

It was already clear quite early in James's reign over both England and Scotland—though Craig did not see this—that Scotland would suffer from having an absentee king more concerned with the problems of his larger and richer kingdom than with those of his smaller and poorer one, and that in addressing himself to the task of managing England he would inevitably lose the sensitivity to local situations, born of deep understanding, that he had displayed in Scotland, while his sensitivity to the Scottish situation would progressively diminish as he lost personal contact. 'Here I sit,' he told both houses of the English Parliament in his speech of 1607, 'and govern [Scotland] with my Pen, I write and it is done, and by a Clearke of the Councill I gouerne Scotland now, which others could not doe by the sword.' It was true, and it did not mean that James consciously neglected his northern kingdom. 'And for my part,' he said in the same speech, 'when I have two Nations vnder my government, can you imagine I will respect the lesser, and neglect the greater?' But government 'by a Clearke' was government at long distance, and inevitably aroused Scottish suspicion that it was government in the interests of England. This problem did not grow any easier of solution when James was succeeded by kings who were English in upbringing and feeling and who had none of James's own intimate understanding of the Scottish character and Scottish ambitions both secular and ecclesiastical.

The form which the Reformation took in Scotland presented the King with special problems in that country. John Knox had boldly confronted Queen Mary with the view that it was for the spokesmen for the will of God to judge the behaviour of princes, while Andrew Melville had argued before the young James that Church and State formed 'Two Kingdoms' and that in the former, Christ's Kingdom, the King was not a king or a lord but only a member, and as such was subject to its discipline. George Buchanan, James's tutor, had presented the view that the King's role was to enforce the will of God and that a king who acted unjustly, against God's will, broke his implicit contract with the people and therefore could rightly be removed. And it was the Church, not the King, that was qualified to interpret God's will.

The Scottish Parliament of 1560 adopted Knox's Confession of Faith but rejected his *Book of Discipline*, and this rejection led Knox to organize the Church separately from the political establishment, with its own General Assembly (consisting of both clerical and lay members) guiding the Church's development. In the General Assembly the small middle class was able to voice its claims against Court and Parliament (the latter by the end of the sixteenth century consisting of members of the nobility and representatives of the freeholders of each shire, some uninfluential representatives of the royal burghs elected by the burgh councils, and a clerical representation whose identity was the subject of constant debate after 1560). Although the Reformation in Scotland was effected by elements of the Scottish Baronage, more and more it came to represent new forces in society that the essentially feudal structure of Lowland Scotland found itself unable to accommodate. The small middle class of the town and the neighbouring lairds responded with a special sense of dedication to the Reformation preachers' precisely formulated Calvinist theology and programme, a wholly different attitude from the simple anti-clericalism, the greed for church lands, or the nationalist desire to reject the influence of Catholic France that had variously motivated many of the Protestant nobility. Calvinism in Scotland was not anti-monarchist; but it wanted a king who would accept the authority of God as defined in Scripture, and the problem was, as James at once saw, who was to judge of the correct interpretation of Scripture. Throughout the seventeenth century the more ardent reformers in Scotland sought for a king committed to the view of kingship expounded by Knox and Melville. This fact, and the fact that they never found one, explains most of the troubles and conflicts within seventeenth-century Scotland and helped set in course the train of events that was to end by facilitating a complete union of Scotland and England.

In Scotland after 1603 James continued his struggle to tame the General Assembly and to restore the traditional prestige and power of bishops. He was able to arrange the timing and locality of meetings of the General Assembly in order to give larger representation to conservative northern members (the most ardent Presbyterians came from southern Scotland) which in turn enabled him to secure the approval of the kind of measures he wanted: this policy culminated in 1610 when a General Assembly in Glasgow, containing a large number of northern representatives, approved the transference of certain powers from presbyteries to bishops; in the same year three Scottish bishops were consecrated at Westminster by English bishops. After 1612 James's plans for the Church in Scotland included changes in the method of worship originally prescribed in the Book of Common Order of 1560, and eventually he was able to get a General Assembly at Aberdeen, after much discussion, to produce a Prayer Book that resembled a simplified form of the English one. He had more trouble with the other measures designed to bring Scottish worship closer to the Anglican form. But he knew when not to push too hard, and he ended his reign with the Scottish ecclesiastical establishment reasonably peaceful.

Charles I succeeded his father in 1625. Though born in Scotland, he had left there as an infant and so had none of James's intimate knowledge of the country and its problems. It is not therefore surprising that, although he inherited in England problems with the Puritans and with Parliament that his character and behaviour could only exacerbate, it was in Scotland that the crisis between Charles and his subjects first erupted into civil war. James's introduction of episcopacy in Scotland had left the Presbyterian framework of church government undisturbed, and many of the bishops were not eager to encourage the kind of high church ritual or the *mystique* of episcopacy that James believed supported his own authority and made it easier to use bishops for his own political purposes. James in the end was content to leave it at that, but Charles pressed forward with a full programme of sacramental and ritualistic worship and an authoritarian episcopacy. When he came up to Scotland for his coronation in 1633 he brought with him William Laud, made Archbishop of Canterbury that year, introduced into the royal chapel at Holyrood a service in the English style, established an episcopal see at Edinburgh, and ignored the views and petitions of Scottish ministers. The Scottish Parliament which met during his stay, having had its business carefully prepared in advance by the committee known as Lords of the Articles (an already well established device in Scotland for directing Parliament in the way the King wanted it to go), passed a massive series of Acts implementing Charles' view of what the Church of Scotland (as in England) should be. Charles refused to accept a Supplication from some of the Scottish nobility expressing grievances, and prosecuted one of them, Lord Balmerino, for treason. Balmerino was found guilty by eight votes to seven and, although he was then pardoned, the trial aroused immense anger.

Even greater anger was aroused among Scottish Presbyterians by Charles's stubborn insistence on imposing on the Church of Scotland, without reference either to the General Assembly or the Scottish Parliament, a Book of Canons that styled the King the Head of the Church and a new Service Book, popularly known as 'Laud's Liturgy' and seen by many Protestant Scots as Popish in tendency. It was the Scottish laity that were chiefly enraged by these measures, as they showed by rioting both in Edinburgh and Glasgow when the new Service Book was used. The clergy on the whole had come to terms with episcopacy and some aspects at least of the style of worship preferred by both James and Charles.

But, well trained in Calvinist doctrine and Presbyterian procedure, the laity insisted that it was the General Assembly, in which the King could play no significant part, that should determine how God's word was to be interpreted. It was an exacerbated form of the old problem faced by James: both sides agreed that the King should govern in accordance with the word of God, but Charles held that the King, as Head of the Church, had a divine right to say what that word meant, while the Presbyterian laity denied this absolutely.

Confrontation between Charles and his Scottish Presbyterian subjects was now inevitable. The first sign of this was the 'National Covenant' of February 1638: in this the signatories bound themselves to stand by each other in firm defence of the true reformed religion. Although the Covenant also professed loyalty to the King, its absolute opposition to Charles's religious policies for Scotland undermined this. Charles refused any compromise, and the Covenanters were equally adamant. The result was the brief confrontation between the Covenanting forces and Charles's army known as the First Bishops' War, which ended without fighting in the Pacification of Berwick in June 1639. Charles appeared to make concessions but in fact was playing for time. The General Assembly and the Scottish Parliament worked together in legislating for their form of Presbyterianism and made subscription to the Covenant compulsory. A second confrontation with Charles led to the campaign known as the Second Bishops' War in which a Covenanting army defeated the royal forces near Newcastle on 20 August 1640. The English Parliament agreed to the Scots being paid a substantial sum by the English territories they were occupying in order to withdraw.

Meanwhile, Charles's quarrel with his English Parliament was exacerbating the situation there. After a period of personal rule from 1629 to 1640 he was forced to summon Parliament to obtain desperately needed supplies, but Parliament demanded the redress of grievances first, so he dissolved it. After his defeat by the Scots in August 1640 he had to summon another Parliament, the famous Long Parliament, which began its active career in opposition to the King by securing the execution for high treason of Charles' principal ministers, through whom his personal rule had been maintained. In 1643 the English Parliamentary forces sought help from Scotland in their struggle against Charles, and the result was the treaty called the Solemn League and Covenant, an agreement between the two parties cast (on Scottish insistence) in an uncompromisingly religious form. Both Parliaments undertook 'the preservation of the true Protestant reformed religion in the church of Scotland in doctrine, worship, discipline and government, and the reformation of religion in the Church of England according to the Word of God and the example of the best reformed Churches', and the Scots undertook to send a large army into England to be paid for by the English Parliamentarians and used as they decided. Although the immediate aim—the defeat of the royalist army—of the two parties to the agreement was the same, the ultimate aim was significantly different: the English sought simply a civil and military alliance, while the Scots wanted a rigid Presbyterian form of church government totally enforced in both countries. For the English, the definition of such a phrase as 'the true Protestant reformed religion' was a matter for serious debate, as were the social and political implications of any definition. That debate waxed furious, especially among the multiplying sects in the Parliamentarian army. In Scotland the significant groups were now simply the dominant Covenanting Presbyterians on the one hand and on the other those, conspicuous among whom was Montrose, whose objections to the theocratic absolutism of the Covenanting Presbyterians led them to support a moderate royalist party.

By the end of 1647 the English Parliamentarians had become disillusioned with their Scottish allies while the latter were equally disillusioned with the failure of the Solemn League and Covenant to establish Presbyterianism in England. Charles had been defeated at Naseby by Cromwell's New Model Army in 1645 and Montrose had been defeated at Philiphaugh the same year. In May 1646 a desperate Charles gave himself up to the Scots at Newark as the lesser of two evils. Attempts were made to try to persuade him to sign the Covenant, but this Charles would not do, and eventually the Scots, realizing that they could not accept an 'uncovenanted' king, allowed him to be arrested by Cromwell's army. But the Scottish Presbyterians still hoped to persuade the King to recognize their claims, and when he was a prisoner in Carisbrooke Castle they sent three commissioners to meet him there and conclude a secret 'Engagement' promising Scottish support for him if he would agree to establish Presbyterianism in England for three years and suppress the Independents and sectaries who were gathering influence there. Charles baulked at the condition that he should make the Covenant compulsory, but he undertook to have it confirmed by Act of Parliament. So once more a Scottish army marched into England, but this time in support of the King. By now support for the Covenant was waning among the Scottish nobility. The Scottish army crossed the Border on 8 July 1648, to be destroyed by Cromwell on August 17 to 19 at Preston, Wigan and Warrington.

By this time the Independents had ousted the Presbyterians in the English Parliament (Cromwell had them forcibly removed by Colonel Pride in 1648) and the 'Rump Parliament' that remained proceeded to arrange for Charles' trial and punishment. When he was executed in January 1649 it was clear that what had first seemed like a natural alliance between Scottish and English Protestant anti-royalists was now quite impossible. For one thing, the group in control in England now had clearly rejected Scottish demands for an enforced Presbyterian uniformity in church affairs and stood for the independent conscience in ecclesiastical matters and for another the execution of the King, who after all had been solemnly crowned King of Scots in 1633 and had made concessions to Presbyterianism in the 'Engagement', shocked even many militant Covenanters. Six days after Charles's execution the Scottish Estates (the meeting could not be formally a Parliament because there was no King) proclaimed his son King of Great Britain, France and Ireland. The young Charles, far more politically astute than his father, readily agreed to pledge allegiance to both the National Covenant and the Solemn League and

Covenant as a prerequisite to his being accepted as king and receiving the Scottish aid that was his only hope for recovering the Crown of England. So the Scots, under David Leslie, now found themselves in military support of Charles II against the English under Cromwell. Cromwell invaded Scotland, and utterly defeated Leslie's army at Dunbar on 3 September 1650, going on to take possession of Edinburgh and gain control of all Lowland Scotland. Young Charles, having been crowned at Scone, went south with another Scots army hoping to rally English royalists, but he was overtaken and defeated by Cromwell at Worcester on 3 September 1651 and succeeded, after many adventures, in fleeing abroad. Meanwhile Cromwell's General Monck had pushed north to take Stirling and Dundee and complete the conquest of Scotland. Cromwell was now in control of the whole of the British Isles.

Cromwell expelled the Rump Parliament in 1653 and this left himself and the army in control of all Britain. By the 'Instrument of Government' of the same year the supreme legislative authority of 'the Commonwealth of England, Scotland, and Ireland, and the dominions thereunto belonging, shall be and reside in one person, and the people assembled in Parliament: the style of which person shall be the Lord Protector of the Commonwealth of England, Scotland, and Ireland.' A new Parliament was to be summoned, representing the whole Commonwealth, with four hundred members from 'England, Wales, the Isles of Jersey, Guernsey, and the town of Berwick-upon-Tweed' and thirty each from Scotland and from Ireland. A perfunctory attempt had been made to get Scottish agreement to the union. Cromwell sent Commissioners from the Rump Parliament to Dalkeith early in 1652 to present a 'Declaration' calling for union and asking for the consent without discussion of the representatives of the Scottish shires and burghs—the only representatives that were allowed—and Scottish deputies were later sent to London to discuss terms. But in fact the union was imposed on Scotland by conquest.

Such assent as was given to the Cromwellian union in Scotland was grudging at best: whatever the religious or political views of individual Scotsmen, national pride was humiliated. One of the things that especially outraged the Covenanters was the provision for religious toleration. The thirty-seventh clause of the Instrument of Government read: 'That such as profess faith in God by Jesus Christ (though differing in judgment from the doctrine, worship or discipline publicly held forth) shall not be restrained from, but shall be protected in, the profession of the faith and exercise of their religion; so as they abuse not this liberty to the civil injury of others and to the actual disturbance of the public peace on their parts; ...' Supporters of Popery and Prelacy and practitioners of licentiousness under the cloak of Christianity were excluded from toleration, but this did not prevent many Scotsmen from regarding Cromwellian toleration as a bitter blow,'no freedom or favour but more bitter than ... death itself,' as the representatives of Moray put it.

The Scots were riven by deep differences. Some still adhered to the Engagement of 1647, others, known as Remonstrants because they supported a document known as the Remonstrance which stated that the King was to be recognized only 'so farre as he owns and prosecuttes the cause', hated the Engagers even more than they hated the imposed Cromwellian government. Indeed, the Remonstrants, with their highly qualified and conditional support for Charles compared with that given by the Engagers, were encouraged by Cromwell, although they were very much a minority party, and it was from their numbers that he recruited officials in Scotland, thus exacerbating the schism between the two groups.

Cromwell did find some Scots to participate in his government of Scotland; of the seven Commissioners of Justice he appointed to take over the jurisdictions of the Privy Council and the Court of Session, three were Scotsmen. Archibald Johnston of Wariston, one of the drafters of the original Covenant and a leader of the Remonstrants, was given his former position of Lord Clerk Register in 1657 and subsequently joined the English Council of State. But the participation of some individual Scotsmen did not alter the fact that this was a government imposed by conquest. A royalist rising in the Highlands led first by the Earl of Glencairn and then by John Middleton (later the first Earl of Middleton) in 1654 was crushed at Dalnaspidal, and the Cromwellian grip on both Lowlands and Highlands was complete.

General Monck, Cromwell's commander-in-chief in Scotland and a former royalist, kept the Highlands in order with an army that at one time numbered as many as eighteen thousand men before being reduced to about eight thousand, thus achieving what the Stewart kings had been unable to do—make the writ of the central government run throughout the Highlands. He built forts at a number of strategic points including Inverlochy, where Major (later Colonel) John Hill established a reputation for sympathetic and imaginative treatment of the Highland chiefs. Throughout Scotland heritable jurisdictions were abolished, feudal courts dissolved, and justice was impartially administered (largely because, it was later alleged, the imported English judges 'had neither kith nor kin' in Scotland and so were uninfluenced by family prejudice). Cromwell was generous to the Scottish universities (now including the University of Edinburgh, founded in the late sixteenth century) though prejudiced in favour of Remonstrants in making appointments and distributing patronage. The Declaration of Union granted free trade throughout the Commonwealth, but the jealousy of English merchants led them to do all they could to inhibit the activities of any Scottish rivals, who were in any case in no great condition to compete, with their shipping destroyed and a contribution of £6,000 a month exacted from the country for the costs of the occupying army. In religion, although the Presbyterian Kirk no longer enjoyed the power of enforcing doctrine and behaviour, its kirk sessions, presbyteries and synods continued to function. There was toleration of sects, but the general Puritan tone of Cromwell's government was in itself far from uncongenial to the Scottish Presbyterians.

Gilbert Burnet, who became Bishop of Salisbury, was born in Aberdeenshire in 1643 and was a youngster in Scotland during the

Commonwealth period. He was no friend to Cromwell or to Puritan rigidity, but looking back on this time in his *History of his own Time*, he summed it up favourably: 'in no time,' he wrote, 'the Highlands were kept in better order than during the usurpation.' In the country as a whole 'there was good justice done, and vice suppress'd and punished; so that we always reckon those eight years of usurpation a time of great peace and prosperity.' But it *was* a usurpation, and when, less than two years after Oliver Cromwell's death in September 1658, Charles II was restored to the throne and Scotland reverted to the *status quo* as a separate kingdom though sharing the same monarch as England, there was general rejoicing. But Scotland took no part in the recall of Charles, who negotiated only with the English, and from now it was English policies devised by Englishmen in their own interests that were to prevail in Scotland.

3. The Glorious Revolution

The Restoration in Scotland was much more reactionary than it was in England. As it had been achieved on English initiative, with Scotland playing no part in the events which led to the recall of Charles, and as the main objective in Scotland was to get rid of a humiliating usurpation, the Scots were in no position to make conditions. The Scottish Parliament that met on 1 January 1661, with John Middleton, now made an earl, the Commissioner representing the King, did as it was arranged it should do: it restored the Lords of the Articles (who as royal nominees effectively limited the independence of Parliament and asserted royal influence) and restored to the King the sole power of appointing officers, privy councillors and Lords of Session and of deciding when to call Parliament. It wiped out all legislation since the Parliament of 1633 and replaced the lost twenty-eight years of legislation with a great flow of new Acts which had the effect of putting the clock back to the days of Charles I's most active success in influencing Scottish affairs in the way he wanted. Scottish hopes that some sort of Presbyterianism would be established in both countries were brusquely shattered. Parliament passed an Act leaving the religious settlement to the King's discretion, and the following year Charles imposed on Scotland the episcopal system, devised by James VI and Charles I, that had been abolished in 1638.

At the same time the sacramental and ritual elements so dear to both James and his son were not insisted on, and though Charles would not allow a General Assembly the traditional Presbyterian structure of kirk session, presbytery and synod continued, with the bishops working with the synods. This seemed a reasonable compromise, but the enforcement by the restored Privy Council of a requirement that all ministers appointed since the abolition of patronage [presentation to the parish by the landowner] in 1649 should obtain collation [formal appointment to a benefice] by a bishop caused unnecessary disruption and suffering. Some 270 ministers refused on principle to seek episcopal collation and were ejected from their livings as a result. Middleton had no idea that there would be such a reaction, which undermined his influence and reputation with the King. He lost his position as Royal Commissioner in Scotland and was succeeded by the frequently drunken and semi-literate Earl of Rothes.

But Charles's most important minister in Scotland was John Maitland, Earl (later Duke) of Lauderdale, a former Covenanter and Engager who had steadily moved towards the royalist side to fight for Charles II at Worcester in 1651. Charles appointed him Secretary of State for Scotland in 1661, an office he exercised in London while Middeton and then Rothes were in Scotland as Commissioners, but he himself became Commissioner after Rothes was removed from that office in 1667. Lauderdale virtually ruled Scotland for Charles until 1680. He was a skilful manager of men and parties, well educated, vigorous, determined, loyal to Charles and genuinely anxious to serve his country. In the wheeling and dealing in which he engaged in maintaining his position against his enemies (who included Middleton) he was led into a considerable amount of corruption, but he was always conscientious and even passionate in the pursuit of his political ends.

Rothes' period as Commissioner ended after his policy of firm action against disaffected Covenanters, with prohibition of their 'conventicles' or outdoor meetings, often led by 'outed' ministers, had provoked a rising in 1666. The rising started in the southwest, home of the most extreme and fanatical Covenanters, and the group of ill-armed peasants marched towards Edinburgh to be defeated by General Dalyell at Rullion Green in the Pentland Hills. Rothes was now replaced by Lauderdale. A period of ten years of firm and consistent government followed, with Lauderdale

working through the Privy Council where for a time he had the
help of some able and moderate-minded members: John Hay,
Earl of Tweeddale, a former Covenanter and Engager; Alexander
Bruce, Earl of Kincardine, highly intelligent and intellectually
curious; and Sir Robert Moray, whose moderate line had annoyed
Middleton. Moray was a founder of the Royal Society and had a
wide-ranging interest in science.

Lauderdale was not himself a man of committed religious
principle, and tried to make things easier for the 'outed' ministers
and other disaffected Covenanters by issuing Letters of Indulgence
allowing the ministers to return to their parishes if they undertook
to behave in a peaceable and orderly manner. He did not impose
any prayer book and while there were no meetings of the General
Assembly, kirk-sessions, synods and presbyteries continued to
meet. But this attempt to win over the disaffected to a moderate
episcopalianism with a wide range of allowed practices failed with
the committed Covenanters, who regarded themselves as bound
by a covenant with God which required the total repudiation of
anything savouring of what they called Arminianism or Erastianism. The result was a stiffening of the Government's attitude,
with preaching at a conventicle made a capital offence and fines
for absence from church and other indications of disaffection from
the Establishment. In 1678 the Government decided to punish and
tame the Covenanters in the south-west by quartering on them a
body of 6,000 Highland troops and 3,000 Lowland troops. This
involved considerable looting and dispossession and caused
enormous indignation. The brutal murder of Archbishop Sharp
of St Andrews by fanatical Covenanters followed in 1679 and
preceded the rising in revolt of the Covenanters of the west. The
Government sent James Graham of Claverhouse to enforce the
law against the Covenanters, and after a skirmish with an armed
conventicle on 1 June 1679 at Drumclog near Glasgow, which was
won by the Covenanters, the Covenanting army was finally
destroyed on 22 June at Bothwell Brig by a royal army with
troops from England under the command of the Duke of Monmouth. That was the end of the rebellion and the end of any

possibility of power for the Covenanters. It was also the end of Lauderdale's power in Scotland.

Opposition to Lauderdale had been building up in Scotland during the second decade of his commissionership. His and Charles's attempt in 1669 and 1670 to achieve a union of parliaments between Scotland and England aroused immense opposition from a people who still recalled with indignation the Cromwellian usurpation. Lauderdale believed strongly that, unpopular though the measure was in Scotland, it was the only permanent solution to the relation between the two countries, and that union must come about eventually. He got as far as nominating Scottish commissioners to discuss a parliamentary union, but negotiations broke down and were abandoned when the Scots demanded seats for all members of the Scottish Parliament in any future United Kingdom parliament. Charges of corruption and of using taxation for his own profit brought against him in Parliament helped to discredit him, and when Charles found that he could no longer count on the docility of the Scottish Parliament he had Lauderdale dissolve Parliament and then, as a sign that he was going to govern Scotland more directly himself, recalled Lauderdale and sent his own brother and heir James, Duke of York, to Scotland as Commissioner.

Meanwhile the extreme Covenanters, though powerless after Bothwell Brig, and hunted mercilessly among the hills of south-west Scotland, where their numbers were strongest, became ever more intransigent in their attitude. Their leaders were now Donald Cargill, who was captured and hanged in May 1681 after having excommunicated the King, the Duke of York and the King's Ministers, and Donald Cameron, who gave the name 'Cameronians' to the Covenanting extremists. They had already, in the Declaration of Sanquhar of June 1680, disowned Charles as king for rejecting the Covenants, supporting prelacy and Erastianism and persecuting the godly. They were thus not simply dissenters in matters of religion, but rebels who claimed the right to set up their own separate and independent theocratic state within the existing state, which they did not recognize. The so-called *Queensferry Paper* of 1680 specifically demanded that both church and state be ruled 'not after a carnal manner by the plurality of votes . . . but according to the word of God' (as defined by themselves). James Renwick's *Apologetical Declaration* of 1684 proclaimed open war not only on the Government but on all its officers and supporters. Such intransigence inevitably increased persecution, which in turn bred even further intransigence among the diminishing but unyielding band of fanatical Covenanters.

The Duke of York arrived in Scotland for the second time in 1681, triumphant in his brother's successful manœuvring to stop the English Parliament from passing an Exclusion Bill to prevent him, as a Catholic, from succeeding to the throne. He had at once summoned a Parliament in Edinburgh to secure his succession to the Scottish throne also. He got it to pass an Act asserting that no religious difference could prevent the lineal heir from succeeding. Parliament then went on to pass a Test Act which was an extraordinary bundle of contradictions: it insisted that all public officeholders apart from the King himself and his immediate family must subscribe to Knox's Confession of Faith that had been accepted by the Parliament of 1560, and at the same time that they should accept the King as supreme governor of the Church and renounce all intention to seek any changes in Church or state. Thus James was willing to establish permanently the old Knoxian form of Protestantism if he could in return not only be recognized as Charles's legitimate heir but also once King (and a Catholic King) have the power to rule the Church in Scotland as he pleased. No wonder the Earl of Argyll—whose father had been executed after the Restoration for his support of Cromwell —offered to subscribe to the Act so far as it was 'consistent with itself'. James, suspicious of the power of this great Scottish Protestant nobleman, seized on the opportunity to get rid of him. Argyll's qualification about the Act's self-consistency was regarded as treasonable, and he was brought to trial and condemned to death. Though he escaped abroad, he was executed later without a further trial after returning to Scotland to support

Monmouth's rebellion against James after the latter's accession to the throne in 1685.

During James's period as Commissioner in Scotland the persecution of the extreme Covenanters, diminishing in numbers but increasingly fanatical in attitude, went on apace. Claverhouse pursued them in the field and the Lord advocate, Sir George Mackenzie of Rosehaugh, prosecuted them when captured. That they were often harshly dealt with is undeniable: there were shootings out of hand and torture as well as fines and confiscations. But the Covenanters were themselves cruel and ruthless against their enemies, and their self-righteous exclusiveness and readiness to inflict death on those they deemed to be on the side of the ungodly are not attractive characteristics. The traditional mythology of innocent, God-fearing Covenanters tortured and murdered at will by the wicked Claverhouse and Mackenzie merely for professing unacceptable views has been increasingly challenged by modern historians. However we interpret it, this is an unhappy chapter in Scottish history.

There was a more positive side to Sir George Mackenzie's work. He wrote works of fiction, moral and political philosophy, history and law, and when he was Dean of the Faculty of Advocates founded the Advocates' Library (now the National Library of Scotland). His legal work, while important, is less so than the contemporary work of James Dalrymple, later Viscount Stair, who became Lord President of the Court of Session in 1671 and whose *Institution of the Law of Scotland*, published in 1681, wove Scots law into a coherent pattern guided by Roman Law. 'Stair's Institutes', as the book was familiarly called by generations of students of Scots law, combining as it did the practical with the philosophical, for the first time gave the body of Scots law status and dignity as a fully worked out national legal system which was able to survive the Union of 1707 independent of English law.

When James inherited the throne on his brother's death in 1685 to become James VII of Scotland and II of England he seemed to have everything going for him. Parliaments in both countries welcomed him and granted him the supplies he needed. He easily put down the risings of Monmouth in England and Argyll in Scotland. Scottish Presbyterianism was helpless; Covenanters were successfully pursued and crushed; the last fanatical organizer of conventicles, James Renwick, was captured and executed in 1688. At the same time James pursued in a variety of ways his steady policy of making both England and Scotland safe for Roman Catholics and of appointing Catholics to high office. In Scotland the Letters of Indulgence he issued to Catholics had logically to be extended to Protestant dissenters, provided, of course, their doctrines did not threaten the state (which ruled out the Covenanters). But these Indulgences, issued 'by our sovereign authority, prerogative royal, and absolute power, which all our subjects are to observe without reserve', were viewed with suspicion by Scotsmen, both because they issued from the royal 'prerogative' (an English concept that traditionally had no counterpart in Scotland) and because James was believed to be using them as a means to his ultimate aim of imposing a Catholic tyranny on the country. The 'outed' ministers were, however, now able legally to return to their parishes, where they used their influence against the toleration of Popery. It was not long, therefore, before the atmosphere of loyal welcome that James found on his accession on both sides of the Border gave way to deepest suspicion. The birth of an heir to James and his second and Catholic wife Mary of Modena in June 1688 seemed to assure a Catholic succession, and it was this that provoked the Revolution.

The Roman Catholic issue was bound up with the constitutional issue, for in order to open public office to Catholics James had to dissolve Parliament and impose legislation in virtue of his ecclesiastical supremacy. It was not the crushed and powerless Covenanters who led the effective objection to this—they after all had objected to all civil government that was not run by the godly—but the bishops and the Episcopalians, as well as the middle classes in the burghs. In both Scotland and England more and more of those who found a Catholic monarch and the constitutional implications of his behaviour unacceptable turned to his nephew and son-in-law William of Orange who had married James's Protestant daughter Mary.

When James fled abroad in December 1688 after William's landing in England shortly before, he left the throne of Scotland empty (though of course he never gave up his own claim to the thrones of both kingdoms). William had been invited to come and take the English throne by a group of English magnates. But Scotland was not bound by the English decision. In fact, for the first time since 1603 Scotland was able to take an independent attitude towards the question of who should be her king. The Stewarts had been legitimate kings of Scotland descended from the ancient Scottish royal house, and the fact that one of them had inherited the English throne could not weaken their claims as kings of Scotland even though it made Scotland dependent on England in many ways. The flight of James and England's invitation to William gave Scotland a new chance to assert her independence as a kingdom. It did not necessarily have to choose as its new king the same one that England had chosen. There were many in Scotland who, in spite of everything, regarded the departed James as their lawful king. The Scottish Episcopalians were not keen to have a Dutch Calvinist on the Scottish throne. The English Parliament proclaimed William and Mary joint sovereigns of England in February 1689, and then proceeded to settle in their own favour the terms governing the relationship between king and parliament. Would the Convention of Estates (not a Parliament since there was no king) that met in Scotland the following month take the same course?

There was a Jacobite (pro-James) and a Williamite party in the Convention. A Williamite President, the Duke of Hamilton, was chosen by a small majority. Claverhouse, now Viscount Dundee, rode off in disgust with a group of sixty horses to organize a Jacobite army in the Highlands. The Convention, freed from pressure from Claverhouse and his Jacobite force, finally proclaimed on 11 April 1689 that King James VII had forfeited the Crown of Scotland ('being a profest Papist' and having 'by advice of Evil and Wicked Counsellors invaded the Fundamental Constitution of the Kingdom, and altered it from a Legal, limited Monarchy, to an Arbitrair and Despotick Power') and resolved 'that William and Mary, King and Queen of England, France and Ireland, Be, and Be Declared King and Queen of Scotland'. In this declaration was included a 'Claim of Right' 'vindicating and asserting' the nation's 'ancient Rights and Liberties'. Among the points made in the Claim of Right are that 'by the Law of this Kingdom no Papist can be King or Queen of this Realm'; that 'all Proclamations asserting an absolute Power' in matters of religion 'are contrary to Law'; that 'the imposing of Oaths without Authority of Parliament is contrary to Law'; that imprisonment without trial, the enforcing of 'old and obsolete Laws upon frivolous and weak Pretences', the use of torture in trials, the quartering of troops in private houses, are all contrary to law. It also stated that 'Prelacy and the Superiority of any Office in the Church, above Presbyters, is, and hath been a great and insupportable Grievance and Trouble to this Nation, and contrary to the Inclinations of the Generality of the People, ever since the Reformation...and therefore ought to be abolished.' The Claim of Right also asserted the right of subjects to petition the King, and asked for frequent parliaments 'and the Freedom of Speech and Debate secured to the Members'. The Convention then set out 'Articles of Grievances' which effectively repudiated the whole machinery of government set up since the Restoration, denounced much of the legislation of that period and in particular declared 'that most of the Laws Enacted in the Parliament, Anno 1685, are Impious and Intolerable Grievances' (they included a reassertion of the Test Act, an Act against conventicles, and an Act ratifying and re-affirming the episcopal government of the Church). Neither in the Claim of Right nor in the Articles of Grievances was there any mention of the Covenant.

So Scotland was choosing her king on her terms. Yet the officers sent down from Scotland to administer the oath to William and Mary were curiously reluctant to insist on any conditions. They were instructed by the Convention simply to read over the Claim of Right to them and to present the Articles of Grievances to William, for him to read at leisure and presumably for him to act on or not as he thought fit. The oath they administered included an undertaking to 'maintain the True Religion of CHRIST JESUS, the preaching His Holy Word, with the due and right Ministration of the Sacraments, now Received and Preached within the Realm of Scotland' as well as to 'Abolish and Gainstand all false Religion, contrary to the same' and to 'be careful to Root out all Hereticks and Enemies to the true worship of GOD, that shall be Convict by the True Kirk of GOD, of the foresaid crimes out of our Lands and Empire of Scotland'. William demurred at this, saying that he would not be a persecutor, but he was assured that the words were a mere matter of form; so he signed. What he signed also included a sworn undertaking to 'preserve and keep inviolated the Rights and Rents, with all just Privileges of the Crown of Scotland' and 'to Forbid and Repress, in all Estates and Degrees, Reif [robbery], Oppression, and all kind of Wrong'.

William was not especially interested in or knowledgeable about Scottish affairs, though some Scotsmen in exile had taken refuge at the Hague under his protection and he brought them back with him. They included William Carstares, who had fled to Holland after the Covenanters' rising of 1666 and was to become an important ecclesiastical statesman in Scotland, whose moderate presbyterianism was a significant force in civilizing Scottish religious controversy; George Melville (later Earl of Melville), a more extreme Presbyterian, who had supported Monmouth and was to become Secretary of State for Scotland and later Lord Privy Seal; and Gilbert Burnet, later Bishop of Salisbury, an enlightened moderate Episcopalian. In spite of his personal knowledge of three important Scotsmen representing three significant strands in Scottish religion, William was ignorant of much in Scottish history and society; he did not know the Scottish nobles, and he had no knowledge or understanding of the Highlands. In a letter William had sent to the Convention in Edinburgh in March 1689 he showed that he considered England

and Scotland essentially one country and expressed the hope for a speedy union between them:

> We are glad to find, that so many of the Nobility and Gentry, when here at London, were so much inclined to an Union of both Kingdoms, and that they did look upon it as one of the best Means for procuring the Happiness of these Nations, and settling of a lasting Peace amongst them, which would be advantagious to both, they living in the same Island, having the same Language, and the same common interest of Religion and Liberty, especially at this Juncture, when the Enemies of both are so restless, endeavouring to make, and increase Jealousies and Divisions; which they will be ready to improve to their own Advantage, and the Ruin of Britain; We being of the same Opinion, as to the Usefulness of this Union, and having nothing so much before Our Eyes, as the Glory of GOD, the Establishment of the Reformed Religion, and the Peace and Happiness of these Nations, are resolved to use Our utmost Endeavours in advancing every thing which may conduce to effectuating the same.

The enemies William here refers to are chiefly the French, for his aim was to use his power as King of England and Scotland to prosecute his quarrel with Loius XIV. His reference to identity of language totally ignores the Gaelic-speaking Highlands, and he refers to 'the Establishment of the Reformed Religion' as though quarrels about what that reformed religion really was had not played such an important part in recent Scottish and English history. How many of the Scottish 'Nobility and Gentry' who visited William in England really pressed for a 'Union of both Kingdoms' we do not know. But it is interesting that such a union now becomes the declared policy of the King, as it had been of James VI, while James VII, in the instructions he drew up for his son in 1692 to be passed on to him at his (James's) death, insisted that the two kingdoms should be kept separate: 'As to our Antient Kingdom of Scotland, take all care to let no alterations be made in the Government of that Kingdom, . . . 'Tis the true interest of the Crown to keep that Kingdom separat from England, and to be governed by their laws and constitutions.' Jacobitism—support of the exiled House of Stewart—from now on tended to be associated in Scotland with anti-union views, and after the Union was finally effected in 1707 this aspect of Jacobitism became even more pronounced.

The officers sent down from Scotland to administer the oath to William and Mary were the Earl of Argyll, Sir James Montgomery of Skelmorlie and Sir John Dalrymple. Argyll, son of the executed ninth Earl, had been in exile in Holland and accompanied William to England; Montgomery had been an active Covenanter and was one of those who visited William in Holland in connection with the invitation to him to accept the throne of England; Sir John Dalrymple (later Earl of Stair) was the son of Sir James Dalrymple, first Viscount Stair (of *Stair's Institutes*), and though he had served first as Lord Advocate and then as Lord Justice Clerk under James VII he made his peace with William in the expectation of obtaining high office from him in Scotland. Between them these three represented the three estates of the realm, the peers, the barons and the burgesses, though only one section—if an influential one—of Scottish opinion. They were all Presbyterians and what we can now call Whigs, i.e. Protestant anti-Jacobites who supported the Glorious Revolution which drove out James and brought in William and Mary.

William decided to govern Scotland through a Secretary of State, and Montgomery confidently expected the appointment. When William decided instead to appoint a more moderate Presbyterian, George Melville (whom he created Earl of Melville in 1690), the indignant Montgomery went over to the Jacobites— a defection that indicated the precariousness of William's hold even on Scotsmen of impeccable Whig Protestant credentials. Montgomery refused the consolation of the office of Justice-Clerk and founded an opposition political group in Edinburgh known as 'The Club' which at first consisted both of Whigs disappointed of office under William and of Scottish patriots worried about the preservation of Scottish rights and privileges; it later had dealings with Jacobites also. In this combination of dissident Whigs, Jacobite Tories and Scottish nationalists there emerged the possibility of an inter-party Scottish Jacobitism as well as a coalition against any proposal of a complete union between Scotland and England.

William's policy in Scotland did not increase his popularity there or bring his ideal of union any nearer fulfilment. Claverhouse, with Highland support, led a Jacobite rising and won the battle of Killiecrankie in July 1689 against a government force led by General Hugh Mackay of Scoury, but his death at the moment of victory ended the threat from that quarter and it looked as though William was now firmly in control of all Britain. But the Highlands remained a problem, as was regularly pointed out to him, for there were significant elements of Highland society that remained loyal to James. Why they remained loyal to a royal house that for generations had either neglected them or regarded them simply as a nuisance to be kept under control by one means or another, is a question that deserves some attention, for it concerns an important point about the elements that made up Scotland's sense of nationhood.

Some of the Highland clans continued to regard James as their lawful king covertly or overtly until the final defeat of the Jacobite movement at Culloden in 1746. The reasons for this were partly religious—parts of the Highlands remained Catholic, if sometimes only nominally—and partly social and political. In the Highlands a feudal system of land tenure, first organized by the Anglo-Norman element in Lowland Scotland, came up from the south to challenge the older patriarchal system. The feudal system gave rights to the owner of the land, while in the older patriarchal system personal status and familial relationships meant everything. The feudal superior, with his rights of feudal jurisdiction, was not necessarily the patriarchal chief, and feudal charters granting land ownership were suspect in the eyes of clansmen who had been brought up to believe in the rights of kindred rather than of legal ownership. A hereditary monarch was the natural superior of a clansman living in a patriarchal society, while a feudal landowner coming between him and the monarch represented a kind of superiority that puzzled him. The clansmen consistently exerted themselves to gain freedom from existing feudal superiorities and to prevent the establishment of new ones, and they associated this freedom with loyalty to the hereditary monarch. Those chiefs, notable among whom were the Earls of Argyll, who employed the devices of feudal law to gain possession of the territory of other clans, drove a wedge between two elements in the Highlands. They for the most part accepted the Revolution of 1689, while the others, who were in the majority, did not and continued to regard the Stewarts as the legitimate hereditary kings of Scotland whose claims they could understand in the light of their own familial organization. They tended to see James as the king who understood their social organization and who stood for a direct relationship between king and chief against the oppressive mediate figure of the feudal superior.

James recognized this in some degree. In the letter of advice that he left for his son he said that 'the body of the Nobility and Gentry, and the Gen: of the Commons are very loyal and Monarchical especially the Com: be north Forth and all the Highlands, except the Campbells'. This was an exaggeration: there were other Highland clans besides the Campbells who supported the Revolution of 1689 and were to support the Hanoverian government in the next century: they included those whose territory was too far from that of the Campbells to have been threatened by their manœuvres—the Mackays, Sutherlands and Munroes. Some clans, notably the Mackenzies, Mackintoshes, Gordons and Grants, remained divided among themselves. The Macdonalds were the great Jacobite clan, and the Camerons, Macleans, and Appin Stewarts also shared their distrust of the Campbells and their sympathy for the Jacobite cause.

One might have expected the Highlands to be influenced by the fact that William's co-sovereign Mary (for both countries had offered the crown to William and Mary jointly) was the daughter of James VII and an authentic Stewart. Since in old Celtic Scotland the transmission of a right through the female was recognized (that was how Bruce became Earl of Carrick), it is surprising that Mary's position was ignored in the Highlands. But the fact is that the clansmen had turned against recognition of succession through the female line because of their resentment at feudal manoeuvrings whereby the daughter of a clan chief who had no sons was married off to a stranger who thus acquired superiority over clan lands. There were many complaints in the Highlands about this practice as one of the many devices employed by wily outsiders to dispossess traditional landowners. In any case, William and Mary left no children, so the question of the right of any son of Mary to succeed never arose. William survived Mary and was in due course succeeded by Mary's sister Anne, a genuine Stewart who reigned in her own right from 1702 to 1714, during which period the Jacobites remained quiescent, hoping to see her succeeded by her half-brother, who was the son of James's second, Catholic wife and was brought up with his father in exile in the conviction that he was the true heir to the thrones of both Scotland and England

It was William's attempt to solve the Highland problem that led to his greatest blunder in the Highlands. He was persuaded by his Secretary of State for Scotland, Melville, to accept into his Government George Mackenzie, first Viscount Tarbat, a former minister of Charles II who was now anxious to prove himself to William by demonstrating his ability to pacify the Highlands. Tarbat's plan was simply to buy peace among the clans by distributing among them a sum of 'five or six thousand pounds', but Claverhouse's success in raising a Highland army for James frustrated this plan. John Campbell, first Earl of Breadalbane, another Stewart supporter who had gone over to William, who prided himself on his knowledge of the clans, then undertook to distribute the money and received a commission from William 'to meet, treat and correspond with any of the Highlanders in order to reduce them to submission and obedience'. But time went by and nothing was done, while Jacobite activity in the Highlands persisted. Then early in 1691 William again commissioned Breadalbane to treat with the Highland chiefs. The Secretaryship for Scotland was now held jointly by Melville and Sir John Dalrymple (though soon afterwards Dalrymple succeeded in ousting Melville and getting the job for himself). Dalrymple and Breadalbane worked together in their Highland scheme, each in his own interest—Dalrymple wanting the pacification of the Highlands as a preliminary to a complete union of Scotland and England, while Breadalbane was seeking to make his branch of the Campbells the most powerful and important in the country.

Breadalbane met the chiefs at Achallader in Argyllshire in June 1691 and succeeded in persuading them to agree to refrain from any hostilities until the following October, by which time it was expected that the exiled James would have sent a message to those chiefs who were loyal to him absolving them from their allegiance in the interests of their safety. But Breadalbane was suspect in the Highlands: both his character and his motives were mistrusted. Alasdair Macdonald of Glencoe, known as MacIain, Chief of Clan Iain Abrach, was particularly suspicious. Now in his sixties, he had fought for James with Claverhouse at Killiecrankie, while his clan had a long record of depradations and raids both against the Lowlands and against other Highland clans, notably the Campbells. They had given trouble by raiding at least since the sixteenth century.

On 17 August William issued a statement pardoning, indemnifying and restoring all who had been in arms against him provided they took an oath of allegiance to him before 1 January next. James, in exile, hesitated to send a letter absolving the chiefs from their allegiance to him, and without such a letter many of them would not subscribe to the oath to William. The letter finally arrived late in December, just after Dalrymple had become sole Secretary of State for Scotland. Dalrymple deliberately decided to take advantage of the situation to destroy the Macdonalds of Glencoe, whom he regarded as the worst of the trouble-makers. By 1 January 1692 most of the chiefs had taken the oath to William, after a proclamation announcing 'the utmost extremity of the law' against those who failed to meet the deadline. One by one they came before the Sheriff of the county, as the law required, to subscribe the oath. MacIain heard of James's letter of release late in December, and came to Colonel Sir John

Hill (who, as we have seen, had a long record of sympathy with the Highlanders), the veteran military governor at Inverlochy. Hill pointed out to him that the oath had to be administered by the Sheriff of Argyll at Inverary. After a hard journey in bitter weather MacIain arrived at Inverary on 2 January, but found that the Sheriff was on the other side of Loch Fyne, on his estate in Ardkinglass, celebrating the New Year with his family. He returned on 5 January and, after berating MacIain for his lateness, administered the oath to him on the 6th: MacIain swore allegiance to William's Government on behalf of himself and his people. It was five days after the Government's deadline.

Dalrymple, however, was determined to make an example of MacIain and prepared plans with Breadalbane for punitive action. He authorized Sir Thomas Livingstone 'to march our troops which are now posted at Inverlochy and Inverness, and to act against these Highland rebels who had not taken the benefit of our indemnity, by fire and sword and all manner of hostility'. William read and signed this document, together with a further document, presented by Dalrymple on 16 January, promising indemnity for Glengarry, who had also delayed in taking the oath, once he had given up his arms and sworn allegiance, but saying that if MacIain and his clan could be separated from the rest it would be 'a proper vindication of the public justice to extirpate that sept of thieves'. Though Dalrymple heard on 30 January of MacIain's submission, he refused to recognize it and wrote to Livingstone that he was 'glad that Glencoe did not come in within the time prescribed'. He wrote of his plans to Colonel Hill: 'let it be secret and sudden'. But Hill was old, and known to be sympathetic to the clans, so Dalrymple planned his attack on the Macdonalds of Glencoe not with him but with his second-in-command Lieutenant-Colonel James Hamilton and Major Robert Duncanson of the Argyll Regiment. The man put in charge of actually carrying out the destruction of the Macdonalds of Glencoe was Robert Campbell of Glenlyon, a sixty-year-old impoverished drunkard whose land had previously been raided by the Macdonalds. On 1 February Campbell arrived at Glencoe with two companies of the Earl of Argyll's regiment, whom, with MacIain's agreement, he quartered among the people of Glencoe. They had come as friends, they said, and wanted quarters till the bitter winter weather improved. They were welcomed as friends and treated as guests under the sacred Highland code of hospitality. But at five o'clock on the morning of 12 February the guests suddenly turned on the hosts with the intention of murdering every single one of them. MacIain himself was shot; men, women and children were shot and bayoneted to the number of thirty-eight; the rest managed to escape in the early morning winter darkness into the snow-covered hills.

This was the infamous Massacre of Glencoe, for which Dalrymple must take prime responsibility, though William, who signed the authorization, cannot be held guiltless. News of the massacre naturally strengthened Jacobite feeling among the clans. William had lost any chance he might have had of uniting Scotland behind his Government. But the sad truth about the massacre is that it was an act of savage revenge planned by Scotsmen against Scotsmen and reflected the rift in Highland society that had in considerable measure originated in the policy of earlier Stewart kings of building up Argyll as a power great enough to dominate the other clans in the interests of the Government.

Other events in William's reign turned many Scotsmen against him. The most important of these concerned the fate of a new Scottish trading company. The English Navigation Acts of 1660 and 1663 had excluded Scotland from any participation in England's profitable trade with Asia, Africa and America. Even in England the East India Company jealously preserved its monopoly. In the early 1690s the idea arose that a company based in Scotland, established by act of the Scottish Parliament, would enable Englishmen and Scotsmen together to break the East India Company's monopoly. The upshot was the 'Act for a Company Trading to Africa and the Indies' passed by the Scottish Parliament in 1695. This Act, which received the royal assent, set up a trading company called 'The Company of Scotland

Trading to Africa and the Indies' and gave it many privileges, including a permanent monopoly in Scotland of trade with Asia and Africa and a thirty-one year monopoly in America. A capital of £600,000 was fixed, with half assigned to England. But the English never subscribed anything, for they were actively prevented by the intervention of the East India Company and their agents. Pressure groups representing English merchants persuaded both the English Parliament and William to act against the Scottish plan. The Scots were forced to act on their own, and in anger and pride they managed to raise £400,000 themselves, an incredible sum for such a poor country. They needed a further £200,000 which they tried to raise abroad, but again were prevented by English agents. Thus shut off from trading in Africa, India and America and prevented from raising money outside Scotland, the company decided to found a trading colony on the Isthmus of Darien, which connects North and South America and separates the Caribbean Sea from the Pacific Ocean. It was regarded as a natural centre of world trade.

The so-called 'Darien Scheme' was destroyed by the English and the Spanish. Spain claimed the territory where the Scottish expedition settled in 1698 and attacked the settlers continuously. The English Government sent a circular letter to all their colonial officials asking them to ensure that no supplies reached the Scottish colonists. After great suffering the survivors of four Scottish expeditions to Darien were forced to give up, and in March 1699 they set off for Scotland in four ships, three of which sank in a storm while a fourth fell into the hands of Spain. Though William, on the urging of Lord Seafield who was now Secretary for Scotland, interceded with Spain for the release of those captured—they had been sentenced to death as pirates—he did nothing whatever to help the Darien colonists or the Scottish company, and refused to approve an Act asserting the Scottish colonists' right to settle in Darien.

That was the end of the Darien Scheme and a great blow to the Company of Scotland Trading to Africa and the Indies. Scottish indignation against the English, and often against William personally, rose to new heights, for it was they and they alone who were held responsible for the disastrous failure of what had been considered so promising a scheme. At the same time it was clear, at least to some, that while England and Scotland pursued conflicting trading policies relations between the two countries would steadily worsen. There were those in both Scotland and England who more and more began to think that only a complete union between the two countries could solve this problem, by giving Scotsmen access on an equal footing with the English to English colonial markets and introducing complete free trade across the Border. At the same time many Scotsmen felt angered with and humiliated by the English and were not in any mood to consider them as other than the traditional enemy. And the Jacobite Highlands had grievances of their own. It looked as though the main political division among Scotsmen was going to be between Unionists and Nationalists. The matter was made more complicated—and more urgent—by the question of who should succeed to the throne on the death of William and Mary's successor, Queen Anne.

4. *Arguments and Manœuvres*

Mary died childless in 1694, and William died in 1702. In England the Declaration of Right of 1689 had settled the crown on Mary's sister Anne, who had deserted her exiled father and her much younger half-brother James to support the Protestant succession. She was married to the ineffective George of Denmark, brother of the Danish king, and although she bore him seventeen children only one survived infancy, but died in 1700. In Scotland the Claim of Right had similarly designated Anne as heir to the throne if Mary failed to produce offspring. The English Parliament went further, and by the Act of Settlement of 1701 settled the Crown of England on Sophia, Electress of Hanover, and her descendants. Sophia was the daughter of Elizabeth, Queen of Bohemia, and granddaughter of James VI and I, who was Elizabeth's father. In the event, it was Sophia's son George, Elector of Hanover, who succeeded on Queen Anne's death in 1714: George was, through the female line, great-grandson of James VI and I.

The Scottish Parliament was not involved in the English Act of Settlement and deliberately left open the question of the succession after Anne as long as possible. This was a matter of continuous annoyance and apprehension to English politicians, who feared that Scotland might recall the Stewart line or in some other way invite a king who would threaten the stability of the English Crown. From now on it became a major object of English state policy to close the 'back door' to England by ensuring that Scotland had no alternative but to choose the same line of succession to the Scottish throne as had been settled for the throne of England. And the most effective way to ensure that would be a complete union of the two countries. In such a union—an 'incorporating union', in the terminology of the age—England as the larger and more powerful country would inevitably call the tune, to an even greater extent than she had done after the Stewarts inherited the English throne and ruled both countries from England.

Anne succeeded in both countries without any fuss. The Jacobites accepted her as a temporary expedient, while hoping that on her death her half-brother James, whom they considered as the true heir and who was twenty-three years younger, would be brought to the throne. In June 1702 the Scottish Parliament, 'Considering, That by the Decease of the late King William of ever Glorious Memory, the Crown and Royal Dignity of this Kingdom is, according to the Claim of Right, and by undoubted Right of Succession devolved upon Queen ANNE; And that Her Majesty hath duly sworn the Coronation Oath, conform to the said Claim of Right', and in view of the proclamation of her succession by the Scottish Privy Council, formally recognized her right and title. It went on to pass an Act 'for Securing the true Protestant Religion, and Presbyterian Government', which declared that the Queen, 'with Advice and Consent of the Estates of Parliament', ratified, approved and permanently confirmed all Acts against Popery and in favour of 'the True Reformed Protestant Religion' that had been passed by Parliament and specified that accordingly the government of the Church of Scotland should be 'by Kirk-sessions, Presbyteries, Provincial Synods, and General Assembly'.

This was the same Parliament that had brought William to the throne of Scotland, re-assembled by Anne and her ministers because it seemed favourable to union and could be counted on to grant supplies. But its legality was questionable, not only because it had not been re-assembled within the prescribed time but also on the grounds that after the death of one monarch and the accession of another a fresh election should have been called and a new Parliament elected. The fourth Duke of Hamilton, who had fought for King James against Monmouth and was now principal parliamentary spokesman for Scottish national feeling, refused to recognize this meeting of the Estates as a true Parliament, 'for as much as by the fundamental laws and constitutions of this kingdom, all Parliaments do dissolve by the death of the King or Queen'. He led a considerable group of members out of the House, members of the Country Party, consisting largely of Presbyterians whose Scottish national feeling had been outraged by events in William's reign, and Jacobites. In their absence the Commissioner, the second Duke of Queensberry, a man dedicated for his own reasons to the union of Scotland and England, was able to get the remaining 120 members (mostly Whig Presbyterians) to pass an 'Act Enabling her Majesty to Appoint Commissioners to Treat for an Union betwixt the Two Kingdoms of Scotland and England'. But they were still a little nervous about the consequences for the religious establishment in Scotland, and immediately after voting for this Act they sent a letter to the Queen emphasizing their concern that, whatever the Commissioners should eventually recommend, there should be no change in the Church of Scotland. They reminded her of what had been said about this in the Claim of Right and concluded by expressing the hope 'that your Majesty, both in the nature of the Commissioners, and in the whole Procedure of the Treaty, will have a Gracious and Careful Regard, to the maintaining of the Presbyterian Government of the Church, as now established by Act of Parliament, and Ratified by Your Majesty in this Session of Parliament'.

'The Act for the Union', wrote Sir David Hume of Crossrigg in the valuable diary he kept of Scottish parliamentary proceedings between 1700 and 1707, 'is only a power enabling the Queen to name Commissioners to meet, treat, and consult with the Commissioners for England, and to set down their articles in duplicates, one for the Queen, one for the Parliament of Scotland, and 2 for the Parliament of England.' But these articles were never set down, for the two sets of Commissioners—one from Scotland and one from England—could not agree. They first met at Westminster on 10 November 1702 and soon got bogged down in arguments about trade. The Scots agreed to accept the English Act of Settlement on condition that the English granted Scotland certain freedoms and privileges in the matter of trade. Some progress was made in agreeing on details of free trade between the two kingdoms, but when the Scots demanded that the privileges of their company trading in Africa and India should be preserved intact and, when this was denied, went on to demand compensation for the dissolution of the company, the English Commissioners resisted. The English Commissioners had not, in fact, been keen on the discussions from the beginning, and were dilatory and negligent during the meetings—so much so that after the Commission had been adjourned eight times for lack of an English quorum it was found necessary to reduce the quorum from thirteen to seven. The Government wanted union for political reasons—to ensure that Scotland accepted the Act of Settlement and to close the back door into England—but English trading interests were suspicious of it on commercial and financial grounds: they did not want impoverished Scots gaining any of their privileges or having access to their markets. Deadlock was reached by the end of January and on 3 February a letter from the Queen was read adjourning the session until 4 October. But by this time the Scottish Parliament, incensed with the Commissioner for refusing royal assent to an Act for securing the liberty of the kingdom, decreed the Commission to be 'terminate and extinct'. So instead of adjourning until October the Commission came to an end in February.

Such was the end of the first move towards union in Queen Anne's reign. It was clear now that the matter needed further parliamentary debate on both sides and that fuller agreement on the Scottish side on certain fundamental political issues was required before progress could be made. This meant a new Scottish Parliament, whose legality was beyond doubt, in which the basic issues could be thoroughly ventilated and in which the Court Party, as the Queen's ministers and their supporters were called, would—they hoped—by the judicious bestowing of honours and exercising of influence and by the making of appropriate deals with relevant parties, see their wishes for an incorporating union finally fulfilled. The tenth Earl of Argyll had already received a dukedom and James Ogilvie, Viscount Seafield, had received an earldom both as rewards for earlier support of the Government and to encourage its continuance. But in fact the Scottish Parliament that first met on 6 May 1703 was to prove surprisingly independent and intractable and its proceedings the most exciting in the whole of Scottish parliamentary history. The abolition of the Lords of the Articles in 1690 had given the Scottish Parliament a new kind of life and independence, and its final years were its finest.

The debate about union had already been going on outside Parliament. In 1702 the Whig Presbyterian journalist George Ridpath published his *Discourse upon the Union of England and Scotland* in which he recalled earlier proposals for union, especially those made in the reign of James VI, which he discussed at length, and argued that all proposals for union made before the Union of the Crowns were more favourable to Scotland than those put forward since. For 'ever since that time to the beginning of this Reign there has been a prevalent Party in that Court, who have been for imposing on us in relation to both Church and State, and instead of allowing us a share in any thing of their Constitution, which was better than our own, they have been for obliging us to a Compliance with that which was worse than our own'. The main reason for this, he argued, was the following:

> The Union of the Crowns was thought sufficient to answer the main Design of the Courtiers, which was to shut up Scotland, as a Back-door for Invasions upon them from France or elsewhere; and not only so, but Scotland being under the same Sovereign, they knew that we must be oblig'd to be Partakers with them in any War they should afterwards happen to be engag'd in; and if upon any occasion we prov'd refractory, they doubted not but the Court Party at home would be able with their assistance to bring us to a Compliance: and therefore since we were tied to the same Line of Succession with England, they did not think themselves oblig'd to make us the same

Tenders towards a Union, that they did, when we liv'd under a distinct Sovereign. Thus it came to pass, that the Proposals of uniting the Nations were not only neglected, but ridicul'd both in the Parliament of England and in their Convocation; and the greatest Outrages imaginable were done to the Honour of Scotland by satyrical envenom'd Reflections: the Privileges which had formerly been allow'd us by the Common Law of England were denied us, and the Court being engaged in a Design to overthrow our Religion and Liberty, the Methods beforemention'd were agreed upon to pursue and effect it, and the High Church Party, as they are call'd, did all they could to enable the Church to accomplish it.

This state of affairs, Ridpath argued, had gone on throughout the seventeenth century, and even King William, 'one of the best of Kings, and a Prince that came in designedly to redress our Grievances', was influenced in the same direction by his advisers, who led him to treat the Scots 'in the Matter of our East India and African Company, and Darien Colony' in a way that 'can certainly never be forgotten while we continue as a Nation'. He went on to cite other English acts against Scottish trade in William's reign, including 'an excessive Imposition laid upon our Linen Cloth, equal almost to a Prohibition'.

Ridpath was in favour of union, but only under terms that would fully guarantee the traditional rights of Scotsmen and their full equality with the English. He considered that the proposals for union made by the English in the reign of Edward VI were much better than anything put forward since. These were to bring the two nations together 'under one Head, in a perfect Equality and Amity'; to have 'a mutual Intercourse of Merchandise, and all Laws prohibiting the same abolished'; to have both nations 'enjoy their own Laws and Customs'; and to make it lawful 'for the subjects of either Nation to trade in the other, or the Dominions thereunto belonging, by Export or Import, by Sea or by Land'. And he went on to make specific proposals, including the requirement of the consent of both Parliaments in making peace and war and forming alliances (for Ridpath's idea of union precluded a union of Parliaments); that the sovereign and his Court should reside in Scotland one year in three 'that the Sovereign may be the better acquainted with the Constitution of the Country, by which means they will secure the Affections of our People, and have an opportunity of doing so by redressing our Grievances in Person'; and 'that we be restor'd to such Parts of our Constitution as we have been depriv'd of by the Union of the Crowns, and particularly to that necessary part of it, of having our Parliaments chuse their own President; of having our Judges Officers of State and Privy councellors chosen in Parliament, and accountable to the Parliament for their Administration'.

These were the views of an anti-Jacobite Whig Presbyterian patriot who had already shown his passionate Scottish patriotism by translating from the Latin a work by Sir Thomas Craig (whose work on the union of the two kingdoms we have already examined) published in 1602, under the title *Scotland's Soveraignty Asserted*. This was 'A Dispute concerning HOMAGE, against those who maintain that Scotland is a Feu, or Fee-Liege of England, and that therefore the King of Scots owes Homage to the King of England'. Though later in the century events were to associate Scottish nationalism primarily with Jacobitism (accurately illustrated in Scott's character Redgauntlet), at this time there was also a strong anti-Jacobite Presbyterian form of nationalism, which took a very cautious attitude indeed towards proposals for union. The most eloquent and passionate, as well as the most original in his political thought, of the anti-Jacobite nationalists was Andrew Fletcher of Saltoun, whose important role in the debates on the Union we examine in the next chapter. Another anti-Jacobite nationalist was Lord Belhaven, who was also to play a notable part in the union debates. Ridpath, Fletcher and Belhaven all agreed that ever since 1603 Scotland had been *imposed upon* by English interests with respect both to Church and State. These three were at the opposite extreme from the Jacobites in their view of monarchy (indeed Fletcher seems at heart to have been a republican), yet on the question of union they were to have much Jacobite support.

The new Parliament met for the first time on 6 May 1703. The preceding seven years—the 'seven ill years' as they were called—had been years of appalling summer and autumn weather and blighted harvests. In 1698 Fletcher of Saltoun had appealed to Parliament to 'take into their consideration the condition of so many thousands of our people who are, at this day, dying for want for bread', and the situation had grown worse since then. While politicians debated the rights and wrongs of union, the rural population of Scotland were in deepest distress: it is said that of parishes in Midlothian 300 out of 900 persons died of starvation and throughout the country thousands of livestock were destroyed. There was thus an acute economic dimension to Scotland's problems in the opening years of the eighteenth century. Fletcher, for all his passionate concern for Scottish nationality, was equally concerned with social problems and the economic plight of rural Scotland, as his two discourses on the affairs of Scotland, both written in 1698, clearly reveal. At the same time, one consequence of the 'seven ill years' was to impress on many Scottish politicians that any union that would be of use to Scotland must have real economic advantages for the country.

The parliamentary election for the 1703 Parliament showed three main parties contending with each other in Scotland: the Court Party, representing the English Government and the Queen's ministers; the Country Party, also known as the Patriotic Party, led by the Duke of Hamilton and supported by Fletcher of Saltoun, two men who were less concerned with religious differences (otherwise so strong in Scottish political life) or with the traditional demarcations between factions, than with obtaining full recognition of the sovereignty and traditional rights of Scotland, believing that any union with England should guarantee these as well as equal trade privileges with England; and the Jacobites, who agreed with the Country Party in demanding free trade with England and a policy for Scotland freed from English interests but differed from that party in looking to young James (son of the exiled James VII, who had died in 1701) as the true heir to the throne of both countries. Many of the Jacobites were Episcopalians, but often less committed to their religious position than the Whig Presbyterians.

Sir George Mackenzie of Tarbat, created Earl of Cromarty and Viscount of Tarbat on 1 January 1703, had been appointed Secretary for Scotland (jointly with Queensberry) on Queen Anne's accession. In 1703, before the opening of the new Scottish Parliament, he sent her two papers analysing the political situation in Scotland. He emphasized that the Presbyterian Whigs were at bottom less favourable to monarchy than the Tories and defined Whig and Tory as follows:

> ... Whig in Scotland hath a very different signification from what it hath in England; for by Whig I understand a party who principaly oun a design for parity in church Government by presbytry and are enimys to what is opposite to that, for, tho they be not against monarchy absolutely, yet it hath but the second place in their esteem. In this party there are two classes, the one who think presbytery of a divine right, and with those it is a principal head of their religion, and all concerns must cede to it: others of them, tho they esteem it much, yet they will not readily either fight or suffer for it: those are less enimys to monarchy than the first, which is truely inconsistent with monarchy or any government which will not be subjected to their mode of hierarchie or common-welth of pop's.
>
> Tory, in general, signifies all who are opposite to Whig, wherin there is one class who place both their religion and their interest in bringing in the P. of Wales [the exiled young James] by whatever method or assistance; the other class of them are firm to the monarchy and to the true line in the Protestant religion. The greatest part of these are indifferent as to church governments, provided they encroach not on the monarchy, and be not of a persecuting principle against any of the reformed religion.
>
> In these senses and significations the Tories are thre to one amongst the vulgar, and four to one amongst the nobility and gentry. Whig will oun the monarch so long as monarchy ouns them, and, when it does not, they will fly in its face, in arms, if they can, and, if they can not, by preaching.
>
> Tory will not resist the monarchy, but will not assist it much,

whilst it is joined with Whig and supports them, but will very willingly subject the Whig to monarchy.

In these circumstances, Tarbat argued, it would be safer 'if her Majesty place her Ministry in the Tories hands' for then 'she will be sure of the greatest part of the nation, they being a party who are zealous for monarchy, and can easily beare with any church government, which will be subject to the soveraign.' He went on: 'They will beare with presbytery, the Whig cannot beare with prelacy; they will frankly allow tolleration to Whigs clergy; nay, more, that the government of presbytery be continued to their clergie, so that the Episcopal clergie be but tollerat amongst the people and parishes of that principle, albeit Whig will never acquiesce nor willingly submit to Episcopacy, tho it were by law established.' He concluded that 'the Queens Government will stand upon a broader and more natural base in the Tories hands than in the Whigs'.

Queen Anne acted on this advice at least to the extent that during the elections to the 1703 Parliament Tories and indeed Jacobites were wooed by the Government. Although in the new Parliament Queensberry was again Commissioner and the Lord Chancellor (roughly the equivalent of the modern Speaker) was the Earl of Seafield, all the more extreme Whig ministers were dismissed. Tarbat himself, as joint Secretary, represented the traditional Tory monarchist view: in Charles II's time he had consistently supported the Government's policy in Church and State. Tarbat's brother, Mackenzie of Preston-Hall, was appointed Lord Justice-Clerk; the Earl of Tullibardine became Lord Privy Seal and later (having succeeded his father as Marquis of Atholl) Duke of Atholl. Seafield assured the Jacobites that if they recognized Queen Anne and supported the Government against the Country Party they would be tolerated as Episcopalians and allowed to have a share in the conduct of affairs, and an indemnity was issued for all acts of treason since the Revolution.

We can get a Jacobite view of these proceedings from the *Memoirs of the Affairs of Scotland, from Queen Anne's Accession to the*

Throne to the Commencement of the Union of the Two Kingdoms of Scotland and England in May, 1707, by George Lockhart of Carnwath. This powerfully Jacobite-oriented account of the events that led up to the Union of 1707 takes us to the heart of the great debate, and, partisan though it is, it gives the facts accurately enough. Lockhart's vivid character sketches of the principal actors in the drama stand out among contemporary literature of the subject. Here he is on Seafield: 'He was finely Accomplished; a Learned Lawyer, a Just Judge; Courteous, and Good-Natur'd; but withall, so intirely Abandon'd to serve the Court Measures, be what they will, that he seldom or never consulted his own Inclinations, but was a blank Sheet of Paper, which the Court might fill up with what the pleas'd.' One of his most generous sketches is that of Fletcher of Saltoun, Member of Parliament for Haddingtonshire, who shared Lockhart's Scottish patriotism though he had no sympathy with his Jacobitism:

> Being Elected a Parliament Man, in the Year 1703, he shew'd a Sincere and Honest Inclination towards the Honour and Interest of his Country. The thoughts of England's Domineering over Scotland, was what his Generous Soul could not away with. The Indignities and Oppression Scotland lay under, gaul'd him to the Heart. So that in his Learned and Elaborated Discourses, he exposed them with Undaunted Courage, and Pathetical Eloquence. He was Bless'd with a Soul, that Hated and despised whatever was Mean and Unbecoming a Gentleman, and was so Stedfast to what he thought was Right, that no Hazard nor Advantage, no not the Universal Empire, nor the Gold of America, could tempt him to yield or desert it.

This is how Lockhart saw the parties in the Parliament which first met in June 1703:

> At the time when the Parliament met there were different Parties or Clubs, First, The Court Party, and these were Subdivided into such as were Revolutioners, and of Antimonarchichal Principles, and such as were any thing that would procure, or secure them in their Employments and Pensions, and these were Directed by the Court in all the Measures. Secondly, the Country Party, which consisted of some (tho' but few) Cavaliers [the Jacobites now called themselves

the Cavalier party], and the Presbyterians, of which the Duke of Hamilton and the Marquis of Tweeddale were leaders. Thirdly, the Cavaliers, who, from the House they met in, were call'd Mitchel's Club, of whom the Earl of Home was the Chief Man.

The Government, in view of their concessions both to Tory feeling and to the Jacobites (whose calling themselves Cavaliers indicated their favourable response to the Government's overture), and the diminished numbers of the Country Party that were returned to this Parliament, considered themselves assured of majority support. It never occurred to them that the Cavaliers and the Country Party would unite in opposition to certain Government proposals, although this, as we shall see, is what happened. The Opposition in this Parliament looked naturally to the Duke of Hamilton, Scotland's premier duke, a puzzling character whose vacillations were to bewilder both his friends and his enemies. It has been argued that, since he had a legitimate if distant claim to the Crown of Scotland, he did not want to see either the restoration of the Stewarts or the accession of the House of Hanover, and that this accounts for some of his hesitancies and inconsistencies. He also had large debts, and heavily encumbered estates in England, which made him vulnerable. But at this stage nobody doubted his opposition, on patriotic grounds, to an incorporating union with England.

Although we may define the parties and the aims and policies of those most active in each, the fact remains—and it was one of the most intractable problems faced by the Government since 1689—that the most influential Scottish peers, the 'magnates', were usually found playing for their own hand, in rivalry with each other, and tended to co-operate with the Government only to the extent that their own interests would benefit. The 'management' of Scotland involved playing one Scottish magnate against the other without alienating any of them, and from the beginning of William's reign it had become increasingly clear that Scotland was becoming unmanageable. The four principal magnates on the scene in 1703 were the Dukes of Hamilton,

Queensberry, Atholl and Argyll; of these Queensberry was the most unremittingly self-seeking, trying to make himself indispensable to the Government in his own interest. Lockhart of Carnwath was, of course, a prejudiced witness (he regarded Queensberry as 'the first Scots Man that deserted over to the Prince of Orange, and from thence acquir'd the Epithet (among Honest Men) of Proto Rebel' and accused him of 'having undertaken and promoted every Proposal and Scheme for Enslaving Scotland, and Invading her Honour, Liberty, and Trade, and rending her Obsequious to the Measures and Interest of England'); but he was not far out when he said that Queensberry would stop 'at nothing to advance his own Interest and Designs'. He used the Court Party and the Court Party used him. The other magnates also played for their own hand in their own way, thus making it difficult to trace any clear ideological pattern in their behaviour. All this was the direct result of there being two kingdoms under one Crown, with the real power based and the significant decisions made in England. If the problem of the English Court was how to 'manage' Scotland, that problem provided an opportunity for the Scottish magnates, as Dr P. W. J. Riley has recently pointed out, to play the system for what it was worth and make what they could out of it. In the light of all this, it may seem surprising that the debates on union in Scotland's last Parliament were so passionate and principled. Such speeches, however, were not as a rule made by the magnates but by independent-minded individuals such as Fletcher of Saltoun, Lord Belhaven and George Baillie of Jerviswood.

At the very time of the opening of the new Parliament there appeared an anonymous work entitled *An Historical Account of the antient Rights and Power of the Parliament of Scotland*, which was in fact by George Ridpath. It argued, somewhat unhistorically, that traditionally Scotland's monarchy was always limited by the ultimate sovereignty of Parliament, and its main objective was clearly to influence members in their discussion of conditions under which the successor of Queen Anne to the Scottish throne should be invited. Indeed, the author specifically said that he humbly offered his treatise 'to the consideration of the Estates when they come to settle limitations for the next successor'. 'Limitations' were the great argument among Scottish patriots: the word referred to the purely Scottish terms that would be insisted on before any successor to Queen Anne would be accepted. That such terms were held to involve limitations on the royal power to prevent such power being used in England's rather than Scotland's interests indicated the way the Opposition was thinking. But it is interesting that the Cavaliers, who looked back with longing to the Stewarts who had been exiled for asserting their prerogative in too absolute a way, and the Country Party were drawn by a common nationalism into agreeing on curbing the power of the next monarch. This is one of many paradoxes involved in the great debate on union which raged from 1703 until 1707.

Parliament opened on 6 May 1703 with the traditional riding in procession from Holyrood to Parliament House. This old feudal ceremony of 'riding the Parliament' had last taken place in 1685, since that of 1689, being a Convention and not a true Parliament, did not ride. Whether or not there was any awareness that this was the last time the picturesque old ceremony was to take place, there was more than usual pomp on this occasion. It was indeed a historic procession, the last acting out of an ancient traditional pageantry, the last opening of Scotland's last Parliament. John Hill Burton, in the eighth volume of his *History of Scotland*, published in 1898, put together an account of this occasion from contemporary sources:

> The first operation was to have the long street from the Parliament Square to Holyrood House cleared of dirt and impediments—a task of some difficulty and importance. A proclamation was issued, prohibiting the use of miscellaneous vehicles within the gates of the city during the ceremony, and for preserving strict order in the crowd. A passage through the centre of the long street was railed in: and, while the magistrates provided a civic guard to the extremity of their dominion at the Nether-Bow Port, the royal foot-guards lined the remainder of the street to the palace gate. . .

The first movement of the day was by the officers of state, who proceeded one hour before the rest of the members to arrange matters for their reception. The Lord High Constable, with his robe and baton of office, and his guard ranged behind him, sat at the Lady Stairs, by the opening of the Parliament Close, to receive the members under his protection, being officially invested with the privilege and duty of the exterior defences of the Parliament House. He made his obeisances to the members as they dismounted, and handed them over to the Lord Marischal, who, having the duty of keeping order and protecting the members within the House, sat at the door, in all his pomp, to receive them.

The procession, according to the old feudal usage, began diminutively, and swelled in importance as it went. The representatives of the burghs went first; then, after a pause, came the lesser barons, or county members; and then the nobles—the highest in rank going last. A herald called each name from a window of the palace, and another at the gate saw that the member took his place in the train. All rode two abreast. The Commoners wore the heavy doublet of the day unadorned. The nobility followed in their gorgeous robes. Each burghal commissioner had a lackey, and each baron two, the number increasing with the rank, until a duke had eight. The Nobles were each followed by a train-bearer, and the Commissioner was attended by a swarm of decorative officers, so that the servile elements in the procession must have dragged it out to a considerable length. . . . All the members were covered, save those whose special function it was to attend upon the honours—the crown, sceptre, and sword of state. These were the palladium of the nation's imperial independence, and the pomp of the procession was concentrated on the spot where they were borne—the same as they may yet be seen in Edinburgh Castle—before the Commissioner. Immediately before the sword rode the Lord Lyon, in his robe and heraldic over-coat, with his chain and baton. Behind him were clustered a clump of gaudy heralds and pursuivants, with noisy trumpeters proclaiming the approach of the precious objects which they guarded. Such was the procession which poured into that noble oak roofed hall, which still recalls by its name [Parliament House] and character, associations with the ancient legislature of Scotland.

. . . Instead of the arrangement by parties, with which we are familiar in the British Houses of Parliament, the Estates were distributed according to ranks. They all sat in one house, and appear to have been much nearer in form to the French States-General, whose latest meeting had welcomed the accession of Louis XIII, than to the English Parliament. The Chancellor sat as chairman, and the officers of state clustered round him on what were called the steps of the throne. Raised and decorated benches at the upper end of the hall were for the exclusive use of the nobles, . . . In the centre was a table, round which were seated the judges of the Court of Session and the clerks of Parliament. Beneath this, on a series of plain benches, or forms, were ranged the lesser barons and burgesses; and strangers specially admitted sat at the extremity of these seats. Beneath the bar there was sometimes a motley assemblage of the attendants of the higher members and state officers, and it would seem that the miscellaneous public, unless on special occasions, had access there.

This then was the scene at the opening of Scotland's last Parliament, whose final Act was to vote itself out of existence. But before that Act was passed there took place one of the most remarkable series of debates, manœuvres, protests, clashes, and tergiversations in the history of any Parliament.

On the opening of Parliament on 6 May 1703, the Queen's letter was read, recommending prudence and unanimity in the discussion of measures necessary for the security of the kingdom and the encouragement of trade and warning against animosities and embittered differences. The Duke of Hamilton then introduced an Act recognizing Anne as the legitimate heir of William, thus implying that the 1702 Parliament, which had also passed an Act recognizing Anne, was invalid, but Hamilton did not go on, as some thought he had intended, to attack the validity of the 1702 Parliament. On the second reading on 15 May the Lord Advocate, Sir James Stewart, proposed the addition of a clause 'That it is, and shall be High Treason in any of the Subjects of this Kingdom, to Disown, Quarrell, or Impugn Her Majesty's Right and Title to the Crown of this Kingdom', and this was carried with the help of the Cavaliers.

Lockhart of Carnwath points out in his account of the proceedings that many blamed Hamilton and the Cavaliers 'for complying with the Court in this point' adding: 'but in my Opinion, they may easily be justify'd, considering that this was the particular piece of Service the Queen demanded of them, in recompence of the great Things she promised to do for them; and with what confidence could they have expected to be admitted into her favour, and entrusted with the Administration of Affairs, if they had oppos'd her in it; if she and her Servants broke their Engagements afterwards to them, that was not their fault, . . .'

It looked as though the Court was going to have everything its own way, especially when on 19 May the Earl of Home, by previous arrangement with Queensberry (in the words of Sir David Hume of Crossrigg), 'gave in a motion by way of Act, for a supply, all blank in the sum and time'. But immediately the Marquis of Tweeddale, representing the Country Party, proposed a counter motion that made clear that all was not to be plain sailing for the Government after all. The motion resolved that before all other business 'the Parliament might proceed to make such conditions of government and regulations in the Constitution of this Kingdom to take place after the decease of Her Majestie and the heirs of her body as shall be necessary for the preservation of our religion and liberty'.

The Government (or the Court, as contemporary writers generally called the Queen's Ministers and their supporters) and Queensberry on its behalf were desperately anxious to have the Act of Supply passed, for it provided the necessary taxation without which the Government could not be run, while the Opposition were determined to use it as a major weapon in wringing concessions favourable to Scottish nationhood. On 26 May Queensberry tried to persuade the supporters of Tweeddale's motion that if they voted the Act of Supply there would be plenty of time given later for discussion of religion and liberty. To this 'it was said they might very much rely upon the Commissioner's word, but what if contrary orders should come from Court, it was known the Treasurer of England behoved to be consulted on our affairs before the Queen were acquainted' (Hume of Crossrigg). Hume went on to report that the Duke of Hamilton 'had a great elogy on the Treasurer of England as a very worthy person, that would give no ill advice to the Queen but still Englishmen will give advice with regard to their own country'. Fletcher of Saltoun made the same point even more vigorously. He asserted that an Act of Supply should be the final rather than the initial Act of any session of Parliament, or at least it should 'lie upon the Table, till all other great Affairs of the Nation be finish'd, and then only granted'. He went on (in a speech printed later in the same year among others he made at this session of Parliament):

'Tis a strange Proposition which is usually made in this House; That if we will give Mony to the Crown, then the Crown will give us good Laws: as if we were to buy good Laws of the Crown, and pay Mony to our Princes, that they may do their Duty, and comply with their Coronation Oath. And yet this is not the worst; for we have often had promises of good Laws, and when we have given the Sums demanded, those Promises have been broken, and the Nation left to seek a Remedy; which is not to be found, unless we supply the Laws we want, before we give a Supply. And if this be a sufficient reason at all times to postpone a Mony Act, can we be blam'd for doing so at this time, when the Duty we owe to our Country, indispensably obliges us to provide for the common Safety in case of an Event, altogether out of our power, and which must necessarily dissolve the Government, unless we continue and secure it by new Laws; I mean the Death of her Majesty, which God in mercy long avert? I move therefore, that the House would take into consideration, what Acts are necessary to secure our Religion, Liberty, and Trade, in case of the said Event, before any Act of Supply, or other Business whatever be brought into Deliberation.

This provoked what Hume of Crossrigg called 'long, and tedious, and nauseous repetitions in debate, till candles were brought in', after which the proceedings were adjourned until two days later, 28 May. By this time the Cavaliers had reconsidered their favourable response to the Government's overtures and were moving towards a coalition with the Country Party in what both parties considered the Scottish national interest. In vain the Government's Whig supporters tried to divide the Opposition by introducing questions about toleration and episcopacy and similar matters that might be expected to divide the Presbyterians in the Country Party from the Episcopalians in the Cavalier Party. It was to no avail, and the Commissioner, seeing that the combined votes of Countrymen and Cavaliers would prevail, gave way gracefully and accepted the motion without a vote. It was Fletcher's motion that was carried: 'Resolved that Parliament will proceed to make such Acts as are necessary or fit for securing our Religion, Liberty, and Trade, before any Act of Supply, or any other Business whatsoever.'

This was a significant victory for those who wanted to assert Scotland's right to make her own conditions before accepting any proposals from a Government run, as they believed, in England's rather than Scotland's interest. In spite of the fact that Episcopalians in the Cavalier Party took a very different view of the kind of religion they would like to secure in Scotland from the rigid Presbyterians among members of the Country Party, Cavaliers and Jacobites hailed the passing of the motion with delight. Lockart of Carnwath recorded triumphantly:

> Then the Parliament proceeded to frame and finish such Acts as tended to secure their liberties and Freedom from the Oppression they sustained thro' the Influence of English Ministers over Scots Counsels and Affairs, in which a long time was spent, many bold Speeches, and excellent Overtures being made, the Court strenuously opposing them all; and the Cavaliers, and Country Party, as strenuously Insisting, at last prevailed, and carried in Parliament these Two valuable Acts; First, An Act anent Peace and War; Declaring, among other Things, That after Her Majesty's Death, and failing Heirs of Her Body, no Person, at the same Time King or Queen of Scotland, and England, shall have sole Power of Making War with any Prince, State, or Potentate whatsoever, without consent of Parliament: ... And, Secondly, that Excellent and Wisely contriv'd Act of Security, which has since made such a Noise in Britian.

The commitment of the Cavaliers to join the Countrymen in demands for guarantees for the claims of Scottish nationhood made it clear to Queensberry that an Act of Security guaranteeing such claims could not be prevented: the question now was only what its terms would be. The debates on the Act occupied Parliament from 9 June to 13 August, and it was often fierce on both sides. Sir John Clerk of Penicuik, advocate, antiquary and member of parliament for Whithorn, a Whig who supported union, wrote of the debates in his *Memoirs*: 'At times we were often in the form of a Polish diet with our swords in our hands, or, at least, our hands on our swords.' On 9 June Lord Belhaven, in the words of Hume of Crossrigg, 'had a long discourse on the attempts of Union with England, both before K. James 6., and since, and the kingdom's encroachments ever sence, and their endeavours to exalt the prerogative here, to sett up Episcopacy to enthral us, not on a religious account: He was by some desired to print his discourse'. Parliament then went on to argue about the Act of 1681 which established the successor to the throne as the next in blood in the royal line, whatever his religion. This Act had already been rescinded in the fifth session of the previous Parliament, but this did not prevent some members from arguing that it might clash with the right of the Estates to nominate the sovereign, and the Lord Advocate 'gave in a draught for rescinding the said Act' a second time. After a long debate, in which the more ardent Jacobites in the Cavalier Party opposed the rescinding as the Act would enable them to dispute the succession of the Electress of Hanover, while the Duke of Hamilton and the Country Party supported the rescinding as the most effective way of thwarting equally the claims of both Hanoverians and Jacobites, it was agreed that the motion to rescind the Act should lie on the table.

Hume of Crossrigg's diary, 22 June 1703: 'Given in by the Marq. of Montrose, a Draught of an Act for security of the kingdom; two by the Ld. Advocate, a long one and a short one to the same purpose; one by Salton [Fletcher of Saltoun], containing 12 limitations upon the successor. After long altercation, Agreed these four should be allowed to be printed by the Sollicitor, and given to the Members of Parliament, against next Sederunt.' According to George Ridpath, who published anonymously an account of the proceedings of this session of Parliament in 1704, 'that which was most taken notice of and came nearest to the Act that the House agreed to, was the draught given in by Mr. Fletcher of Salton'. Fletcher's proposed Act contained the famous twelve limitations which laid down the conditions under which the Estates should accept the successor to the Scottish Crown. In his speeches pressing for these limitations, he argued eloquently from history. Prejudice and opinion govern the world, he said, and whole nations are governed by delusions. He went on:

Of these Delusions, one of the strongest and most pernicious, has bin a violent Inclination in many Men to extend the Prerogative of the Prince to an absolute and unlimited Power. And tho in limited Monarchies all good Men profess and declare themselves Enemies to all tyrannical Practices, yet many, even of these, are found ready to oppose such necessary Limitations as might secure them from the tyrannical Exercise of Power in a Prince, not only subject to all the Infirmities of other Men, but by the Temptations arising from his Power, to far greater. This Humour has greatly increas'd in our Nation, since the Union of the Crowns; and the slavish Submissions, which have bin made necessary to procure the Favours of the Court, have cherish'd and fomented a slavish Principle. But I must take leave to put the Representatives of the Nation in mind, that no such Principles were in this Kingdom before the Union of the Crowns; and that no Monarchy in Europe was more limited, nor any People more jealous of Liberty than the Scots. These Principles were first introduc'd among us after the Union of the Crowns, and the Prerogative extended to the Overthrow of our antient Constitution, chiefly by the Prelatical Party; tho the peevish, imprudent and detestable conduct of the Presbyterians, who opposed these principles only in others, drove many into them, gave them greater force, and rooted them more deeply in this Nation. Shou'd we not be asham'd to embrace Opinions contrary to Reason, and contrary to the Sentiments of our Ancestors, meerly upon account of the uncharitable and insupportable Humour and ridiculous Conduct of Bigots of any sort? If then no such Principles were in this Nation, and the Constitution of our Government had greatly limited the Prince's Power before the Union of the Crowns; dare any man say he is a Scots-man, and refuse his consent to reduce the Government of this Nation, after the expiration of the Intail, within the same limits as before the Union? And if since the Union of the Crowns, every one sees that we stand in need of more Limitations; will any Man act in so direct an opposition to his own Reason, and the undoubted Interest of his Country, as not to concur in limiting the Government yet more than before the Union, particularly by the Addition of this so necessary Limitation for which I am now speaking?

Fletcher's limitations were to apply 'in the case only of our being under the same King with England' and were as follows:

1. 'That Elections shall be made ... for a new Parliament every year.'

2. 'That so many lesser Barons shall be added to the Parliament, as there have been Noble-men created since the last Augmentation of the Number of Barons; and that in all time coming, for every Noble-man that shall be created, there shall be a Baron added to the Parliament.' (i.e., increased representation for the shires.)

3. 'That no Man have Vote in Parliament, but a Noble-man or elected Member.'

4. 'That the King shall give the Sanction to all laws offer'd by the Estates . . .'

5. 'That a Committee of one and thirty Members . . . chosen out of their own Number by every Parliament shall during the Intervals of Parliament, under the King, have the Administration of the Government, be his Council, and accountable to the next Parliament; . . . and that in the said Council, all things to be determin'd by Balloting in place of Voting.'

6. 'That the King without consent of Parliament, shall not have the Power of making Peace and War; or that of concluding any Treaty with any other State or Potentate.'

7. 'That all Places and Offices, both Civil and Military, and all Pensions formerly confer'd by our Kings, shall after be given by Parliament.'

8. 'That no Regiment or Company of Horse, Foot, or Dragoons, be kept on foot in Peace or War, but by consent of Parliament.'

9. 'That all the fencible Men of the Nation, betwixt sixty and sixteen, be with all Diligence possible, arm'd with Bagonets, and Fire-locks all of a calibre, and continue always provided in such Arms, with Ammunition sutable.'

10. 'That no general Indemnity, nor Pardon for any Transgression against the Publick, shall be valid without consent of Parliament.'

11. 'That the fifteen Senators of the College of Justice [i.e. Judges of the Court of Session, who at this time sat as of right as members of parliament] shall be incapable of being Members of Parliament, or of any other Office, or any Pension: but the Salary that belongs to their Place, to be increas'd as the Parliament shall

think fit: That the Office of President shall be three of their Number to be nam'd by Parliament, and that there be no extraordinary Lords. And also, that the Lords of the Justice Court [the High Court of Justiciary, the supreme court in criminal cases as the Court of Session was in civil cases: its members were chosen from the judges of the Court of Session] shall be distinct from those of the Session, and under the same Restriction.'

12. 'That if any King break in upon any of these Conditions of Government he shall by the Estates be declar'd to have forfeited the Crown.'

Fletcher continued to argue eloquently for his limitations:

We have this day an Opportunity in our Hands, which if we manage to the advantage of the Nation we have the Honour to represent, we may, so far as the Vicissitude and Uncertainty of human Affairs will permit, be for many Ages easy and happy. But if we despise or neglect this Occasion, we have voted our perpetual Dependence on another Nation. If Men could always retain those just Impressions of things they at some times have upon their Minds, they would be much more steady in their Actions. And as I may boldly say, that no Man is to be found in this House, who at some time or other has not had that just sense of the miserable Condition to which this Nation is reduc'd by a dependence on the English Court, I should demand no more but the like impressions at this time to pass all the Limitations mention'd in the draught of an Act I have already brought into the House; since they are not Limitations upon any Prince, who shall only be King of Scotland, nor do in any way tend to separate us from England; but calculated only to this end, That so long as we continue to be under the same Prince with our Neighbour Nation, we may be free from the influence of English Councils and Ministers; . . . By which means Trade, Manufactures, and Husbandry will flourish, and the Affairs of the Nation be no longer neglected, as they have bin hitherto. These are the ends to which all the Limitations are directed. That English Councils may not hinder the Acts of our Parliaments from receiving the Royal Assent; That we may not be ingag'd without our Consent in the Quarrels they may have with other Nations; That they may not obstruct the meeting of our Parliaments, not interrupt their sitting; That we may not stand in need of posting to

London for Places and Pensions, by which, whatever particular Men may get, the Nation must always be a Loser, nor apply for the Remedies of our Grievances to a Court, where for the most part none are to be had . . . The best and wisest Men in England will be glad to hear that these Limitations are settled by us. For tho the Ambition of Courtiers lead them to desire an uncontrollable Power at any rate; yet wiser Men will consider that when two Nations live under the same Prince, the Condition of the one cannot be made intolerable, but a Separation must inevitably follow, which will be dangerous, if not destructive to both . . . For my own part, . . . before I will consent to continue in our present miserable and languishing Condition after the Decease of her Majesty, and Heirs of her Body failing, I shall rather give my vote for a separation from England at any rate.

Fletcher went on to argue that the limitations he proposed would be advantageous to Kings of Great Britain who, 'when they have bin perplex'd about the Affairs of Scotland, did let fall such Expressions, as intimated they thought them not worth their Application'. The only reason he could imagine why everybody in the country might not like these proposals is 'that being accustom'd to live in a Dependency and unacquainted with Liberty, we know not so much the meaning of the Word'. In concluding this speech, Fletcher repeated his historical argument that 'our Ancestors did enjoy the most essential Liberties contain'd in the Act I have propos'd'. He pointed to 'the low Condition into which we are sunk, and the extreme Poverty, Distress, and Misery of our People' and went on:

Let us consider whether we will have the Nation continue in these deplorable Circumstances, and lose this Opportunity of bringing Freedom and Plenty among us. Sure the Heart of every honest Man must bleed daily, to see the Misery in which our Commons, and even many of our Gentry live; which has no other cause but the ill Constitution of our Government, and our bad Government no other root, but our Dependence upon the Court of England.

Though Fletcher was generally regarded as one of the strong men of the Country Party, he was essentially an independent patriot, whose views did not coincide wholly with those of any political or religious group. His arguments for the limitations, like his later arguments against an incorporating union, were put forward on the purest patriotic grounds:

> To conclude, these Conditions of Government being either such as our Ancestors enjoy'd, or principally directed to cut off our Dependence on an English Court, and not to take place during the life of the Queen; he who refuses his Consent to them, whatever he may be by Birth, cannot be a Scots-man by Affection. This will be the true Test to distinguish, not Whig from Tory, Presbyterian from Episcopal, Hanover from St. Germains [where the exiled Jacobite Court was], nor yet a Courtier from a Man out of place; but a proper Test to distinguish a Friend from an Enemy of his Country. And indeed we are split into so many Parties, and cover our selves with so many false Pretexts, that such a Test seems necessary to bring us into the Light, and shew every Man in his own Colours. In a word, my Lord Chancellor, we are to consider, that tho we suffer under many Grievances, yet our Dependence on the Court of England is the cause of and comprehends them all, and is the Band that tyes up the Bundle. If we break this, they will all drop and fall to the ground: if not, this Band will straiten us more and more, till we shall be no longer a People.

In spite of his earnestness and eloquence in pleading for his limitations, Fletcher was unable to convince a majority of the House of their necessity, and they were rejected by twenty-six votes. But Fletcher's arguments were carried over into the debates about an Act of Security, whose aim was to be essentially Fletcher's aim of making accession to the throne of Scotland after Anne's death subject to conditions that would safeguard the dignity and freedom of the Scottish nation. After many weeks of ardent and sometimes rowdy debate, in which the Act was discussed clause by clause, and a great variety of topics were introduced as the subject of possible clauses, the shape of the Act of Security was finally worked out, and it was approved by about sixty votes, with many abstentions. The question now was whether Queensberry, as Commissioner acting for the Queen would touch the Act with the sceptre to signify royal approval, and thus get the Act of Supply he so desperately wanted, or whether he would refuse, and so prolong the struggle about supply.

The Act of Security begins by providing for the meeting of Parliament in Edinburgh on the twentieth day after Queen Anne's death, or, if there is no Parliament in being at the time of her death, then the members of the last preceding Parliament should meet. Any vacancies caused by death or promotion shall be filled in the usual manner. If Queen Anne leaves a direct heir of her body or a successor lawfully designated by her, the Claim of Right shall be read to that heir or successor and he shall be required to accept its terms. Provision is made for a regency if the heir is under age: the regent or regents will have to accept the same terms. The Act went on to make its central point:

> And further, upon the said Death of Her Majesty, without Heirs of her body, or a Successor lawfully designed and appointed as above, or in the case of any other King or Queen thereafter succeeding, and deceasing without lawful Heir or Successor, the foresaid Estates of Parliament conveened, or meeting, are hereby Authorized and Impowered to Nominate and Declare the Successor to the Imperial Crown of this Realm, and to settle the Succession thereof upon the Heirs of the said Successor's Body, the said Successor, and the Heirs of the Successor's Body, being always of the Royal LINE of Scotland, and of the true Protestant Religion. Providing always, That the same be not Successor to the Crown of England, unless that in this present Session of Parliament, or any other Session of this or any ensuing Parliament during her Majesty's Reign, there be such Conditions of Government settled and enacted, as may secure the Honour and Sovereignty of this Crown and Kingdom; the Freedom, Frequency, and Power of Parliaments, the Religion, Liberty, and Trade of the Nation from English or any Foreign Influence; with Power to the said Meeting of Estates, to add such further Conditions of Government as they shall think necessary, the same being consistent with, and nowise derogatory from those which shall be enacted in this, and any other Session of Parliament during Her Majesty's Reign ... And it is hereby expressly provided and declared, That it shall be high

Treason for any person or persons to administer the Coronation Oath, or be Witnesses to the Administration thereof, but by the Appointment of the Estates of Parliament in manner above mentioned, or to own or acknowledge any Person as King or Queen of this Realm in the Event of her Majesty's Decease, leaving Heirs of her own Body, until they have sworn the Coronation Oath in the Terms of the Claim of Right: And in the Event of Her Majesty's Decease, without Heirs of her Body, until they Swear the Coronation Oath, and accept on the terms of the Claim of Right, and of such other Conditions of Government, as shall be settled in this, or any ensuing Parliament, or added in the said Meeting of Estates, and be thereupon declared and admitted as above; which Crime shall be irremissible without Consent of Parliament.

The vital clause preventing the successor to the Crown of England from being also the successor to the Crown of Scotland unless Scotland's conditions were met had been moved by the Earl of Roxburgh on 16 July. (Roxburgh, wrote Lockhart of Carnwath, 'was a Man of good Sense, improven by so much Reading and Learning, That, perhaps, he was the best Accomplish'd Young Man of Quality in Europe, and had so Charming a way of expressing his Thoughts, that he pleased even those 'gainst whom he spoke'.) It contained the essence of Fletcher's limitations and produced furious debate before Fletcher moved that it should be voted on, whereupon Seafield, the Chancellor, said that it was late and Queensberry, the Commissioner, adjourned the session until the next morning at 10 o'clock. 'Then there was a great cry and hubbub,' reported Hume of Crossrigg, 'the Privilege of Parliament and the Claim of Right was encroached upon; and the D. of Hamilton, the E. of Rothes, Marquis of Tweddal, &c., took a Protest thereon, and many adhered, and said they would address the Queen; . . . but afterwards, on second thoughts, when the Commissioner was come out they came out, and went to Pat. Steil's.' The next morning the Chancellor set about pacifying indignant members. He said (as Hume reported), 'There was no intention thereby to incroach upon the Privileges of the House, but it being past 8 a clock, many of the members out, many weary and calling for a Delay, it was thought fitt to adjourn, not to hinder the Debate, but in order to its being reassumed this day.' Fletcher insisted that the adjournment had been illegal, but after considerable discussion feeling died down and the question of the legality of the adjournment was not voted on.

But Seafield and Queensberry still faced the problem of what to do about Roxburgh's dangerous clause, now passed by the House. They sought to replace it with a less dangerous clause, and put up Sir James Stewart, the Lord Advocate, to propose that 'the successors to the Crown of England be not nominate King or Queen of Scotland, unless there be a Communication of trade with England agreed to, Freedom of navigation, and Trading with their plantations, &c., as shall be satisfying at the sight of the Parliament of Scotland'. Fletcher accepted this eagerly, and went on to spoil the official plan by moving that *both* clauses (this one and Roxburgh's) should now be put to the vote together. The Lord Advocate started a diversion by raising a question about seating in the House, which the Commissioner eagerly took up. This matter took up the rest of the day's proceedings.

On 23 July the Earl of Roxburgh moved both clauses, and the Lord Advocate had no option but to do the same, adding to Roxburgh's clause the words, 'unless there be such conditions of government made in this or any other Session of this or any other Parliament during the Queen's reign, or in the Meeting of Estates'. Fierce argument ensued as to which clause should be voted on or whether they should be voted on together. Finally on 26 July a conflated version of the two clauses was passed by seventy-two votes.

Both Seafield and Queensberry knew, even before the final passing of the Act of Security on 13 August, that the passing of the conflated clause would cause displeasure in London. Seafield wrote placatingly to Sidney Godolphin, Lord Treasurer of England, explaining and justifying his manœuvre of adjourning the House on the evening of 16 July. He wrote again after the vote on the 26th insisting on his faithfulness in Her Majesty's service and complaining of the difficulty of getting Parliament to accept a reasonable solution, as 'we are invironed with resolvs, and in any thing against the English succession our opposit partie are strongest'. If Parliament insists on refusing to pass an Act of Supply 'there will be great difficultie to praeserve authoritie amd goverment', yet they made approval of such an Act conditional on the kind of guarantees represented by the offending clauses. While some people in Government circles were prepared to grant free trade with Scotland and a share for Scotland in England's colonial trade in exchange for Scottish agreement to the English Act of Settlement (and this had been the purpose of the clause introduced by the Lord Advocate, which he had intended as a substitute for, not an addition to, Roxburgh's clause), Godolphin was equally opposed to both Roxburgh's and the Lord Advocate's clauses. His over-riding aim was to prevent any legislation by the Scottish Parliament that would establish, even conditionally, a succession to the Scottish throne different from that to the English throne.

On Friday 10 September Hume of Crossrigg noted in his diary: 'The Commissioner had a speech, showing he had instructions from her Majesty to touch all the Acts past this Session, except the Act for Security; and he desired the Parliament might proceed to provide for the security of the Kingdom and support of the Government, with all speed.' Hamilton, Roxburgh and others moved that 'an Address be made to the Queen to give orders to touch the Act; this was much insisted on'. On the 16th, again in Hume's words, 'The Commissioner called for the Acts passed this Session of Parliament, and touched them; and then had a discourse, shewing, That it might have been expected this Parliament would have proceeded to secure the nation by granting a supply to her Majesty, but there being soe much time spent, it was fitt they had a short recess.' He therefore asked the Chancellor to adjourn Parliament until 12 October. In fact, Parliament did not meet again until 6 July 1704. The Act of Security had not received the royal assent.

Lockhart of Carnwath gives the Jacobite nationalist view of what was going on:

> 'Tis needless, and would be endless to repeat, suppose I could, the Discourses that were made *Pro* and *Con*, whilst the Parliament was upon Overtures to secure their Liberties, and redeem the Nation from the Oppression it groaned under: 'Tis sufficient to say, That the Court opposed every Thing that could be proposed for that End, and, in Return, were so baffled in all their Schemes and Designs, That when a Motion was made for Granting a first Reading to the Act for a Supply, the Parliament flew in the Face of it, some Demanding the Royal Assent to the Act of Security, others asking, If the Parliament met for nothing else than to drain the Nation of Money, to support those that were Betraying and Enslaving it? And after many hours warm Debates on all Sides, a Vote was stated, *Whether to proceed to Overtures for Liberty, or a Subsidy?* And the House being crowded with a vast Number of People, nothing, for near Two Hours, could be heard but Voices of Members, and others (it being late, and Candles lighted) requiring Liberty and no Subsidy.
>
> The Throne being confounded with this vigorous Appearance in Behalf of the Country, was at a Stand, and knew not what Hand to turn to: And the Earl of Roxburgh declar'd, If there was no other Way of Obtaining so natural and undeniable a Priviledge of the House as a Vote, they would demand it with Swords in their Hands.

This captures something of the excitement and violence of feeling that prevailed during these debates. But the most passionately reasoned speeches against the Commissioner's refusal to touch the Act of Security were those by Fletcher of Saltoun. He returned to the point many times, but one example of his approach will have to suffice:

> I know 'tis the undoubted Prerogative of Her Majesty, that no Act of this House shall have the force of a Law without Her Royal Assent. And as I am confident His Grace the High Commissioner is sufficiently instructed, to give that Assent to every Act which shall be laid before him; so more particularly to the Act for the Security of the Kingdom, which has already passed this House: An Act that preserves us from Anarchy: An Act that arms a defenceless People:

An Act that has cost the Representatives of this Kingdom much Time and Labour to frame, and the Nation a very great Expence: An Act that has passed by a great Majority: And above all an Act, that contains a Caution of the highest Importance for the Amendment of our Constitution. I did not presume the other day, immediately after this Act was voted, to desire the Royal Assent; I thought it a just deference to the High Commissioner, not to mention it at that time. Neither would I now, but only that I may have an Opportunity to represent to His Grace, That as he who gives readily doubles the Gift; so His Grace has now in his Hands, the most glorious and honourable Occasion, that any Person of this Nation ever had, of making himself acceptable, and his Memory for ever grateful to the People of this Kingdom: since the Honour of giving the Royal Assent to a Law, which lays a Lasting Foundation for their Liberties, has been reserved to him.

But the Commissioner was the servant of the Queen, and the Queen and her Ministers were firmly opposed to the Act of Security and its implications. Seeing the Commissioner adamant in refusing to touch the Act, Fletcher returned to his limitations on 15 September. 'His Grace the High Commissioner having acquainted this House that he has Instructions from her Majesty to give the Royal Assent to all Acts pass'd in this Session, except that for the Security of the Kingdom, 'twill be highly necessary to provide some new Laws for securing our Liberty upon the Expiration of the present Intail of the Crown.' Speaking in support of his seventh limitation (that all places, offices and pensions should be given by Parliament and not by the King so long as Scotland has the same monarch as England) he became very eloquent:

Without this Limitation, our Poverty and Subjection to the Court of England will every day increase; and the Question we have now before us is whether we will be Freemen or Slaves for ever? whether we will continue to depend, or break the Yoke of our Dependence? and whether we will chuse to live poor and miserable, or rich, free, and happy?

He proceeded, in what Hume of Crossrigg called 'a long and learned discourse', to argue that this limitation of royal power existed all over the world, including China. He concluded:

> Having thus shewn some of the great advantages this Limitation will bring to the Nation (to which every one of you will be able to add many more) that 'tis not only consistent with Monarchy, but even with an absolute Monarchy; having demonstrated the necessity of such a Condition in all Empires, which contain several Kingdoms; and that without it we must for ever continue in a dependence upon the Court of England; In the name of God, what hinders us from embracing so great a Blessing? Is it because her Majesty will refuse the Royal Assent to this Act? If she do, sure I am, such a Refusal must proceed from the Advice of English Counsellors; and will not that be a Demonstration to us, that after Her Majesty and Heirs of Her Body, we must not, cannot any longer continue under the same Prince with England? Shall we be wanting to our selves? Can her Majesty give Her Assent to this Limitation upon a Successor before you offer it to Her? Is She at Liberty to give us satisfaction in this Point, till we have declar'd to England by a Vote of this House, that unless we obtain this Condition, we will not name the same Successor with them? And then will not her Majesty, even by English Advice, be persuaded to give Her Assent; unless Her Counsellors shall think fit to incur the heavy Imputation and run the dangerous risque of dividing these Nations for ever? If therefore, either Reason, Honour or Conscience have any Influence upon us; if we have any regard either to our selves or Posterity; if there be any such thing as Virtue, Happiness or Reputation in this World, or Felicity in a future State, let me adjure you by all these, not to draw upon your Heads everlasting Infamy, attended with the eternal Reproaches and Anguish of an evil Conscience, by making your selves and your Posterity miserable.

This eloquent speech 'the Chancellor answered very prettily out of Father le Chese [Lachaise]', as Hume reported. Then the Marquis of Montrose moved 'That the House proceed to their Liberty before granting any supply'. Long debate and 'much clamour' ensued until 'after 9 a clock, Resolved, The House should next Sederunt be upon liberty'. But, as we have seen, on the next day the Commissioner adjourned Parliament.

In spite of his frustrations, Fletcher did have the satisfaction of seeing the House pass in September an 'Act anent Peace and War' that embodied one of his limitations. The essence of this Act was that 'after her Majesty's Decease, and failing Heirs of her Body, no Person being King or Queen of Scotland and England, shall have the sole Power of making War with any Prince, Potentate, or State whatsomever, without Consent of Parliament; and that no Declaration of War, without Consent foresaid, shall be binding on the Subjects of this Kingdom'. This Act did receive the royal assent, in the hope 'to have obtained a subsidy for the Army'.

There was hardly any measure discussed by the Scottish Parliament of 1703 before its adjournment of 16 September that did not relate in some way, directly or indirectly, to the nature of Scotland's nationhood and so to the question of Scotland's relation with England and the kind of union between the two countries that was acceptable to Scotland. It was for this reason that Lockhart of Carnwath regarded this session as the most glorious of all sessions of the Scottish Parliament:

And thus I have gone thro' this Session of Parliament, which did more for Redressing the Grievances, and Restoring the Liberties of this Nation, than all the Parliaments since the 1660 Year of God: And it cannot be thought strange, that Scots-men's Blood did boil to see the English (our inveterate enemies) have such Influence over all our Affairs, that the Royal Assent should be granted or refused to the Laws the Parliament made, as they thought proper; and, in short, every Thing concerning Scots Affairs determined by them, with regard only to the Interest of England; To see Bribing and Bullying of Members, unseasonable Adjournments, and innumerable other Ungentlemanny Methods made use of, to seduce and debauch People from the Fidelity they owed to that which ought to be dearest to them, I mean the Interest, Welfare, and Liberty of their Country and Fellow-Subjects, by whom they were entrusted in that Office. These Considerations, I say, enraged and embolden'd a great Number of Members to such a Degree, that many strange and unprecedented

Speeches were made, Enveighing against, and Exposing the Government, especially by that worthy and never to be enough praised, Patriot Andrew Fletcher, of Salton.

Fletcher may be said to have been the hero of the 1703 session of Parliament, and he was to play an equally heroic part in the remaining sessions of Scotland's last Parliament. In December 1703, with Parliament not sitting, Fletcher had leisure to write an important essay on politics. It was published early in 1704, under the title *An Account of a Conversation concerning a Right Regulation of Governments for the Common Good of Mankind* and takes the form of a letter to the Marquis of Montrose and the Earls of Rothes, Roxburgh and Haddington giving an account of a conversation on politics he had recently had in London with the Earl of Cromarty, Sir Edward Seymour and Sir Christopher Musgrave. At one point in the conversation Fletcher tells his companion why he is so keen on his limitations:

> Now, the ill condition of Scotland, proceeding from these causes; that our money is carried away and spent at court, by those who attend there for places and pensions; they by the influence of English ministers upon our government, we are brought wholly to depend on that court; that by reason of the prince's absence, the laws are not put in execution: I say, these being the causes of our present ill condition, what other remedies can be found, than that the parliament of Scotland should, for the time to come, bestow all pensions and offices, both civil and military; and have power to appoint committees for the administration of the government during the intervals of sitting?

He rejects the counter-argument that this would limit unacceptably the power and authority of the prince and concludes this part of his case by telling the Earl of Cromarty, who had brought forward this counter-argument, that 'I had always thought that princes were made for the good government of nations, not the government of nations for the private advantage of princes'.

At this point the Englishman Sir Edward Seymour enters into the argument, asking whether even if the limitations had been passed, Scotland could hope to enjoy them long 'when your prince may be assisted by the power of a far greater nation, which is highly concerned to take them away?' The conversation continues:

> I cannot think, replied I, that the people of England are obliged by their interest to oppose these limitations in Scotland, unless they think themselves concerned in interest to make us at all times their secret enemies, and ready to embrace every opportunity of declaring ourselves openly for such. But since we are not only become sensible of our present ill condition, but fully understand both the causes and the remedy; to oppose us in the prosecution of those means which are absolutely necessary to attain so just an end, would be no less than to declare open enmity against us. We shall run a great risk indeed, said Sir Edward, in so doing! Sir, said I, no man is more fully persuaded than I am, of the great disproportion there is between the power of one and the other nation, especially in the present way of making war. But you should consider, in declaring yourselves in such a manner to be our enemies, you would drive us to the necessity of taking any power that will assist us, by the hand. And you can in no way avoid so great danger, but by doing justice to yourselves and us, in not opposing any conditions we may make with the successor to our crown.

Then the Earl of Cromarty intervenes to say that 'there was an easy remedy to all these inconveniences: which was an union of the two nations'. Fletcher replies:

> I answered, I was sorry to differ so much from his lordship, as to think the union neither a thing easy to be effected, nor any project of that kind hitherto proposed, to be a remedy to our present bad condition: that the English nation had never, since the union of the two crowns, shewn any great inclination to come to a nearer coalition with Scotland: and that I could not avoid making some remarks upon all the occasions that had given rise to treat of this matter during my time. I have observed, that a treaty of union has never been mentioned by the English, but with a design to amuse us when they apprehended any danger from our nation. And when their apprehensions were blown over, they have always shewn they had no such intention. [He goes on to give examples of this.] Now, as I have

shewn how little the English nation has been really inclined to the
union; so I must acknowledge that the Scots, however fond they
have formerly been of such a coalition, are now become much less
concerned for the success of it, from a just sense they have that it
would not only prove no remedy for our present ill condition, but
increase the poverty of our country.

How, I pray, said the Earl?

I am of opinion, said I, that by an incorporating union, as they
call it, of the two nations, Scotland will become more poor than ever.

Why so?

Because Scotsmen will then spend in England ten times more than
they now do; which will soon exhaust the money of the nation. For
besides the sums that members of parliament will every winter carry
to London, all our countrymen, who have plentiful estates, will
constantly reside there, no less than those of Ireland do at this time.
No Scotsman, who expects any public employment, will ever set his
foot in Scotland; and every man, that makes his fortune in England,
will purchase lands in that kingdom: our trade, which is the bait that
covers the hook, will be only an inconsiderable retail in a poor,
remote and barren country, where the richest of our nobility and
gentry will no longer reside: and though we should allow all the
visionary suppositions of those who are so fond of this union; yet
our trade cannot possibly increase on a sudden. Whereas the expences
I mentioned will, in a very short time, exhaust us, and leave no stock
for any kind of commerce.

A long argument with the Earl of Cromarty follows, in which
Cromarty strongly disputes these conclusions and maintains that
Scotland could gain nothing but economic advantage from an
incorporating union, while Fletcher expands on his original case
with detailed examples, including some taken from Ireland. When
Fletcher, addressing Seymour, proceeds to accuse the English of
ill treatment of Wales, the American colonies and the parts of
France they once ruled, and of using scurrilous expressions about
their competitors ('you can hardly endure the name of a Dutch-
man; and have treated them on all occasions with such scurrilous
expressions, as are peculiar to the generality of your people')
Seymour is provoked to exclaim, 'What a pother is here about

an union with Scotland, of which all the advantage we shall have, will be no more than what a man gets by marrying a beggar, a louse for her portion?' This in turn provokes an ironic outburst from Fletcher, but eventually the argument becomes more philosophical, with Fletcher and Sir Christopher Musgrave discussing the nature of injustice in one country's treatment of another (England's treatment of Ireland is brought in again). Sir Christopher argues that one nation's advantage is bound to be another nation's disadvantage, to which Fletcher replies that 'the true interest and good of any nation is the same with that of any other'. At the end of the discussion, Fletcher comes out with a surprising argument that devolution within the whole of Britain would be the ideal solution:

... do you not think the remoter parts of England injured by being obliged to have recourse to London for almost every thing, and particularly for justice? Do you not think them wronged, in that almost all the treasure of England is yearly laid out in this place, and by that means the substance of the other parts exhausted, and their rents and revenues diminished? ... I am of opinion, that if instead of one, we had twelve cities in these kingdoms possessed of equal advantages, so many centres of men, riches and power, would be much more advantageous than one. For this vast city [London] is like the head of a ricketty child, which, by drawing to itself the nourishment that should be distributed in due proportion to the rest of the languishing body, becomes so over charged, that frenzy and death unavoidably ensue. And if the number of people and their riches would be far greater in twelve cities than now in one, which I think no man will dispute; and that these cities were such as are situated in convenient distances from each other, the relief and advantage they would bring to every part of these kingdoms would be unspeakable.... That London should draw the riches and government of the three kingdoms to the south-east corner of this island, is in some degree as unnatural, as for one city to possess the riches and government of the world ... And if the other parts of government are not also communicated to every considerable body of men; but that some of them must be forced to depend upon others, and be governed by those who reside far from them, and little value any interest except their own, studying rather how to weaken them in order to make sure of their subjection; I say, all such governments are violent, unjust, and unnatural ... So many different seats of government will highly tend to the improvement of all arts and sciences; and afford great variety of entertainment to all foreigners and others of a curious and inquisitive genius, as the antient cities of Greece did.

Fletcher concludes by suggesting that London, Bristol, Exeter, Chester, Norwich, York, Stirling, Inverness, Dublin, Cork, Galloway and Londonderry, as being 'cities that are already considerable' in the British Isles, might perhaps be the centres of regional governments. He puts the matter forward very tentatively, but it is interesting to find that in 1703 an ardent Scottish Nationalist has already anticipated the argument brought forward by some people today against Scottish Nationalism—that it implies regional government throughout the British Isles. Such regional government, in Fletcher's ideal world, would be the best guarantee of a true nationalism operating in the interests of the whole population of Great Britain and Ireland.

Such a view was quite beyond the range of thinking of either Government or Opposition. The battle to decide the nature of Scotland's future relation with England continued to be fought in more conventional terms.

6. Brisk Speeches and Great Heats

With Parliament prorogued, all parties engaged in manœuvring for position before the next session. Lockhart of Carnwath viewed the spectacle ironically:

> The Courtiers again they made as great Haste, and all Parties strove who should outdo one another in Paying their Respects, and shewing their Submission to the Good Will and Pleasure of the Duke of Marlborough and Lord Godolphin; the Queen, indeed, for fashion sake, was soometimes addressed to; but such Application was made to these two Lords, that it was obvious to all the world, how much the Scots Affairs depended on them. I my self, out of Curiosity, went once to their Levies, where I saw the Commissioner, Chancellor, Secretary, and other Great Men of Scotland, hang on for near an Hour, and, when admitted, treated with no more Civility than one Gentleman pays another's *Valet de Chambre*, and for which the Scots have none to blame but themselves, for had they valued themselves as they ought to have done, and not so meanly and sneakingly prostituted their Honour and Country to the Will and Pleasure of the English Ministry, they'd never have presumed to usurp such a Dominion over Scotland, as openly and avowedly to consult upon, and determine in Scots Affairs.

The Government heaped honours on those who had supported it and those it hoped would support it in getting Scottish agreement to the English solution of the succession question. The Marquis of Atholl got his dukedom; Tarbat became Earl of Cromarty; Sir John Dalrymple, Viscount Stair, became Earl of Stair. Atholl had been a supporter of King William but, disappointed in his hope for office, had joined the Country Party. But on Queen Anne's accession he had been made Lord Privy Seal and in the 1703 Parliament (in Lockhart's words) 'he trim'd 'twixt Court and Cavaliers'. In spite of their new honours, both Atholl and Cromarty as well as Seafield now came to an understanding with the Cavaliers, to the indignation of Queensberry, who in consequence felt himself isolated. Queensberry felt he could discredit Atholl and the Cavalier Party by taking advantage of a strange business engineered by the devious and volatile Simon Fraser of Lovat. This was the so-called 'Scots Plot'.

The Scots Plot was a Jacobite conspiracy in which Fraser was involved and in which he deliberately implicated Atholl for reasons of personal revenge. Fraser, who had been flitting between the Jacobite Court of St Germains, England and Scotland, seems to have been playing both ends against the middle. He presented a letter to Queensberry which appeared to implicate Atholl in the plot. Queensberry sent the letter to the Queen, convinced that this would ruin Atholl. But Atholl—in Lockhart's words— 'made use of such solid Arguments, and convincing Proofs to shew the Fallacy of that Letter, That Queen Anne her self could not deny, but that she thought it not Genuine'. Robert Ferguson, a professional political intriguer known as 'the Plotter', was instrumental in exposing the extent of Fraser's double dealing in the matter. Enormous excitement and indignation were whipped up on both sides—on the Government side at the existence of a Jacobite plot to bring the Pretender to the throne, on the side of the Opposition, at the treacherous attempt to frame the Duke of Atholl. Queensberry's plan to discredit Atholl blew up in his face, and it was Queensberry who was (temporarily at least) discredited.

Revelations about the Scots Plot had a direct effect on the course of events leading to the Union. The House of Lords appointed a committee to look into the whole matter. They presented the committee's conclusions in an address to the Queen on 31 March 1704, in which they represented that there had been a dangerous conspiracy to raise a rebellion in Scotland and invade that kingdom with a French army in order to subvert Her

Majesty's Government in both England and Scotland and bring in 'the Pretended Prince of Wales' and that nothing had given so much encouragement to Her Majesty's enemies at home and abroad to enter into 'this detestable Conspiracy' as the uncertainty about the succession in Scotland. They therefore most humbly besought her Majesty to have the succession of the Crown in Scotland settled as it was in England, on the Princess Sophia of Hanover and her heirs. In her reply, the Queen reminded their Lordships that she had already declared to her Scottish subjects her intention of endeavouring to settle the succession in Scotland in this way, adding that this was 'the most effectual means for securing their quiet and that of England, and the readiest way to an entire Union betwixt both Kingdoms, in the perfecting of which it was very desirable no Time should be lost'.

The House of Commons, with its Tory majority, resented the interference of the Lords in this matter. The ensuing quarrel between the two Houses was resolved in favour of the Commons. In February 1704 the Earl of Rothes, the Earl of Roxburgh and George Baillie of Jerviswood, all members of the Country Party untainted with Jacobitism, came to London at Atholl's request to express their sorrow that loyal subjects should have been accused of harbouring disloyal intentions and the alarm felt in Scotland at the proposal attributed (inaccurately) to the Earl of Stair that an Army, paid by England, should be maintained in Scotland and parliamentary government in Scotland should be suspended. They urged the Queen to summon the Scottish Parliament as soon as possible in order to investigate the Plot and in the meantime, to be sure that its deliberations would not be biassed, they asked her to withdraw her confidence both from those concerned in the Plot and from those involved in traducing innocent persons in connection with it. The Queen was impressed by the moderate tone of the three delegates and charmed by their manners. The interview ended with an assurance by the Queen that the Scottish Parliament would be summoned immediately and that the papers relating to the Scots Plot would be submitted to it. She concluded by saying that she was determined that the question of succession should be settled in the coming session in the interest of both the Protestant religion and the security of the Kingdom.

As a result of this interview an agreement was reached whereby the Country Party accepted office in support of the Hanoverian succession and Queensberry (in spite of being backed by the Lords) was replaced as Commissioner by the Marquis of Tweeddale. The Earl of Cromarty remained as sole Secretary for Scotland and Sir James Murray, a Queensberry supporter, was replaced as Lord Register by James Johnston, a Presbyterian, anti-Jacobite Whig who had been Godolphin's chief adviser on Scottish affairs and through whose mediation the agreement between the Court and the Country Party had been achieved.

The Government now hoped that with the support of the Country Party they could achieve their aim of settling the succession question in Scotland as it had been settled in England, on the Electress Sophia and her heirs, and were quite prepared to make some concessions to Scottish feeling in order to achieve this. They were prepared to grant that the Scottish Parliament, or the Scottish Privy Council when Parliament was not sitting, should have to approve appointments to offices in Scotland in return for Scottish acceptance of the Hanoverian succession. This in the eyes of the Government—the so-called 'motley' administration—was a reasonable compromise, although of course it was conceding to Scottish feeling far less than Fletcher's limitations or the Act of Security demanded.

Seafield, who remained as Chancellor in the new session of Parliament that opened on 6 July 1704, wrote to Godolphin (in his inimitable spelling) the day before the opening:

> I have disposed the fare greatest pairt of our Old Pairtie [the Country Party] to concurr in her Mejesties measures, and I am not without hops of success. However, there is a verie great pairtie for the delaying to declair the successor. Some think they should have conditions from England concerning our tread, so by thes national and plausable propositions they increase the number that are for delaying. Others sees the danger of delaying and that conditions of government on the successor may be the foundation of a subsequent treatie with

England, bot of al this mater wee can wreat nothing with any certantie till the members come to toun.

Parliament opened on 6 July, but as many members had not yet arrived in Edinburgh it was adjourned until the 11th. Proceedings opened on the 11th with the reading of a letter from the Queen and speeches by the Commissioner and the Chancellor. The Queen's letter earnestly recommended the settling of the succession in the Protestant line, adding that a long delay in settling it in this manner 'may have very dangerous Consequences, and a Disappointment of it would infallibly make our Kingdom the Seat of Warr, and expose it to Devastation and Ruine'. She added:

> As to Terms and Conditions of Government, with regard to the Successor, We have impowered Our Commissioner to give the Royal Assent to whatever can in reason be demanded, and is in Our Power to grant, for securing thr Soveraignty and Liberties of that Our Ancient Kingdom.

Pointing out that 'We are now in a War', the Queen appealed for the voting of supplies to maintain the forces and provide military and naval equipment.

Tweeddale, the Commissioner, promised in his speech to give Parliament satisfaction in 'rectifying abuses crept into your Constitution or Administration of the Government' and 'removing all Encroachments upon the Soveraignty or Liberties of the Nation'. He too insisted on the importance of 'settling the Succession in the Protestant Line' and emphasized the need for supplies. He added that the Queen had already taken steps to institute an inquiry into the Scots Plot and that 'Her Majesty doubts not but your inquiries into this Plot, or any other practices of the like nature, will end in your laying down solid measures for preventing of them, in time to come'. The Secretary, Cromarty, speaking for the Queen, denied what 'some would persuade others to believe that the Queen has a secret will in the Affair now before us, contrary to her express Will, revealed and declared by Her in her Royal Letter'. He appealed for calm and rational discussion without anger, and concluded with the assertion 'which I think evident without Discourse, That as the Union of Britain is apparently the greatest Politick Good; so, as certainly, and by the infallible Rule of Contraries, a Division of Britain is its greatest Evil: And then, it is a necessary Corollary: Whoever is not for the Union of Britain, may be concluded an Enemy to it.'

After these official speeches, Government supporters in the House were startled by a proposal put forward by William Seton of Pitmedden, junior, 'That this House would stand by and defend her Majesty's Person and Government, without naming a Successor to the Crown of Scotland, during this Session of Parliament, but would agree on such Conditions of Government, to take Effect after her Majesty's Death, as might best conduce to free that Kingdom from all English Influence, to the end the Scots might be in a Condition to Treat with England, about a Federal Union.'

Nothing was done about this resolution on that day (11 July), but on the 13th, after the House had spent the intervening period discussing controverted elections, the Duke of Hamilton further disconcerted Tweeddale by a proposal of a similar nature: 'That this Parliament will not proceed to the Nomination of a Successor, untill we have had a previous treaty with England, in relation to our commerce, and other concerns with that Nation.'

'The Court was much surprized and perplexed,' wrote Lockhart, 'not expecting the Cavaliers would have begun so early on that Subject; and they hoped to have time to gull over some of the Members, with passing a few inconsiderable Limitations.' Fletcher of Saltoun did nothing to diminish the Court's perplexity by rising to support Hamilton's proposal. He 'elegantly and pathetically set forth the Hardships and Miseries to which we have been exposed, since the Union of the two Crowns of Scotland and England in one and the same Sovereign; and the Impossibility of amending and bettering our Condition, if we did not take Care to prevent any Design, that tended to continue the same, without other Terms, and better Security than we have hitherto had'.

The Government's position was succinctly put by the Earl of

Marchmont in 'a discourse, showing the danger of delaying a Nomination. There was a Popish Pretender, backt with the power of France, which should make us concerned in this matter.' But the Government decided to move warily, and on 17 July they put up the Earl of Rothes to propose a motion that they hoped would side-track Hamilton's. It was 'that the Parliament will go in the first place into the Consideration of such Conditions and Regulations of Government as may be proper to rectifie our Constitution, and vindicat and secure the Soveraignty and Independency of the Kingdom, and then the Parliament will take into their Consideration the Resolve offered for a Treaty previous to a Nomination' [i.e. of a successor to the Crown].

Argument then arose about which of the two motions should be put to the vote first. As Lockhart put it, 'brisk Speeches and sharp Repartees were made by both Parties, and great Heats arose, which continued a long Time'. Sir James Falconer of Phesdo remarked ironically 'that he was very glad to see such an Emulation in the House, upon Account of the Nation's Interest and Security' and went on to propose that the two motions should be joined together. Hamilton agreed to this and offered a conjoint motion, of which his own formed the first part and Rothes' the second. Then debate began on whether the two motions should be voted on separately or jointly. Eventually it was carried by 42 votes that the vote should be on the combined resolution, which was then voted on and carried by a majority of 55.

The Government regarded the joint resolution as a threat to their strategy, while the Cavaliers were unanimous in support of it, seeing it symbolically as an assertion of Scottish rights. Lockhart's account of the popular feeling in Edinburgh on the passing of the joint resolution is of course biassed in its note of triumph and perhaps exaggerates in some degree, but captures what must have been an authentic feeling on the part of the populace that its passing was a Scottish national victory over English attempts at domination:

> The Temper and Inclinations of the People were very remarkable
> on this Occasion; for after Parliament was that Day adjourned, the

Members that had appeared more eminently in behalf of the Resolve, were caress'd and Huzza'd as they pass'd in the Streets, by vast Numbers; and the Duke of Hamilton was after that Manner convoyed from the Parliament House to the Abbay, and nothing was to be seen or heard that Night, but Jollity, Mirth, and an universal Satisfaction and Approbation of what was done, and that by People of all Ranks and Degrees.

The position now was that the Government's policy was opposed by both the Cavaliers and the group that has been called the Queensberry Whigs (as distinct from those Whigs who supported the Government, notably the Earl of Marchmont): these two groups had reached agreement to vote together. On 17 July, after the vote on the joint resolution, the Duke of Atholl proposed the setting up of an inquiry into the Scots Plot and this gave Fletcher the opportunity to deplore the encroachment of the House of Lords 'on the Freedom of this Nation' by their presuming to investigate the Plot, 'the greatest step that e'er was made, towards asserting England's Dominion over the Scots Crown'. He then offered a resolution castigating 'the House of Lords Address to the Queen, in relation to the Nomination of their Successor to our Crown; and their Examination of the Plot, in so far as it concerned Scotland and Scotsmen, was an undue Intermeddling with our Concerns, and an Encroachment upon the Honour, Sovereignty, and Independency of this Nation; and that the Proceedings of the House of Commons, were like those of good Subjects to the Queen, and good Neighbours to us.' The Lord Chancellor announced that the Commissioner had written and would again write to the Queen 'to send down the whole evidences relating to the Plot as soon as possible'.

On 19 July the Earl of Marchmont tried to deflect the Opposition by raising fears that the Protestant religion was endangered so long as the succession was not resolved. It was pointed out in reply that a Protestant succession was secured by the Claim of Right. On 21 July Hamilton 'gave in the Old Act of Security, leaving out the clause about the Communication of Trade in respect of the Resolve concerning it, showing the necessity of it, to avoid English Influence'. The Earl of Marchmont countered by saying that there was much talk of English influence which all Scotsmen should avoid, but no talk of the much more dangerous French influence. Hamilton spoke again and said 'That he should be one of the first who should draw his Sword against a Popish Successor, though he did not think this a proper Time, either to settle the Succession, or to consider the Earl of Marchmont's Proposal'. He went on to talk of the House of Lords intermeddling with the affairs of Scotland. The Chancellor then said 'that if the Parliament intended to do nothing but to go from one matter to another, it could not be expected they could long stay together'. 'Then there was a great hubub and crying on both sides' until 'the Commissioner rose and said, Such disorders were very misbecoming, and if they did not settle, he would be necessitate to Adjourn, untill they came to a more calm temper'. (Hume's report.)

When Hamilton's supporters continued to urge the reading of the Act of Security the Commissioner again said 'That he had very ample Instructions in case the Parliament had gone in to the main business in Her Majesty's Letter, but seeing they had entered into a Resolve which put off that for this Session, things were so far altered, that he knew not what he could do, without acquainting Her Majesty and receiving her instructions'. Hamilton thanked him for his candour.

Matters came to a head on 25 July, when the Duke of Hamilton once again moved that the Act of Security might be read, but this time adding it as a clause to the Act of Supply. This was to make perfectly clear that the Government could get their Supply only on terms that safeguarded Scotland's dignity and independence. This procedure, of 'tacking' an urgently desired measure on to a money bill, was not uncommon in England, where the Lords had no power to obstruct a money bill and so could be forced to pass a measure they disliked if a money bill was attached to it. But in the Scottish Parliament, where Lords and Commons sat in a single Chamber, the device was seen as simply obstructive. This point was made by Johnston, the Lord Clerk Register, who conceded that 'the tacking of Acts in England' was reasonable 'because there the Parliament consisted of two Houses, and it was not of design to encroach upon the Soveraignty and to straiten the King, but because of differences between the two Houses . . . But here Parliament sate in one house, and Tacking of Acts might obstruct voting of them both.' It was also 'a straitening of the Queen, who might possibly consent to the one, and not to the other'.

A fierce argument ensued. To continue with Hume's account:

> Salton said, He knew, and could make it appear, that the Register had undertaken to prosecute the English designs for promotion to himself. Reg. said, There could be no Influence but the Place he had, and it was known he had lost a higher place for his concern for his country. Some called, That Salton should go to the bar for accusing a Member. Salton, backed by D. Hamil. said, The Letter by the Queen to the Parliament was written when no Scotsman was about her, and so behoved to be by English influence. The Reg. said, It came up to the Queen from Scotland; that he believed there was no English man would be at the pains to draw a letter. Salton still insisting, Sr. Ja. Hacket said, He was impertinent. Salton said, He that would call him Impertinent was a Rascal. The House being alarmed at such expressions, S. J. Ersk moved Both should be sent to prison. The Chancel. gave a sharp rebuke to both; and it resolved in this, first Sr. Ja. Halket then Salton, Declared they were sorry they said any thing that had given offence to the House, and promised upon their word of honour, they should not take any notice of it else where.

After calm was restored Lord Ross moved that the House should vote two months' supply at once and a further four months' after the Act of Security had received the royal assent. A further motion called for no action on Supply until the Queen had given her assent to the Act of Security. Tweeddale was non-plussed. Finally, he said he would 'have to acquaint her Majesty before he could do anything thereanent'. The Government was now desperate for money. The army in Scotland remained un-paid, and with the threat of a Jacobite rising with French assistance always in the background, the situation was dangerous. Lockhart describes with relish what now happened:

> And now I must tell you, that the Courtiers being all along perswaded of their Power to carry through the Succession, with few Limitations granted in lieu thereof, had not made any Demands, or required Instructions concerning the Act of Security; but now that they were fully satisfied of their Mistake, they were obliged to inform the Queen, that their Measures being quite broke, Matters were come to that Height, She must either allow the Commissioner to grant the Royal Assent to the Act of Security, or resolve to adjourn the Parliament, without obtaining Money to pay Her Troops. The Queen, and Her Ministers of England, considering what a Noise these Animosities betwixt Her two Kingdoms would make in the World, thought it better to satisfy the Desires of the People, by allowing that Act the Royal Assent, than by refusing it, to increase the Divisions, and be obliged to disband the Army; and thereupon the Commissioner having acquainted the House, that he had obtained the Queen's Consent, to pass the Act of Security into a Law, it was soon read, voted, approved, and touched with the Royal Scepter.

So on 5 August 1704 the Act of Security was again read and voted, and this time it was 'touched' by the Commissioner. Immediately the House proceeded to pass by a unanimous vote an Act granting Supply for six months.

On 21 July Fletcher of Saltoun, in line with the resolution to defer the nomination to the succession until after an acceptable treaty, had given in a motion for the nomination of eight commissioners from each Estate to meet with a like number from England at some place on the Borders (to ensure freedom from English influence) to treat on the matter of Union. This had received a first reading on 4 August. Once the Act of Security had received the royal assent and Scottish national feeling had been thus appeased, the House were prepared to consider treating with England on equal terms, so on 8 August the second reading of Fletcher's resolution was proposed since 'it seemed reasonable to condescend on the subject of Treaty before a nomination'. This produced fierce debate. Hamilton moved 'that the nomination might be in plain Parliament'. Lord Belhaven argued that before any nomination the Scots Plot ought to be inquired into, since 'many of the Members were tainted, and till they were cleared, it would be unfitt to name them for commissioners'. He gave details of the Plot and named Hamilton, Queensberry, Atholl, Annandale, Leven, the laird of Grant and himself as requiring to be cleared before they could be acceptable to the Commissioners of England.

Bitter altercation ensued. Hamilton said 'that it was necessary to clear the nation of the Plot; that not only those named, but all who voted for the Act of Security last Ses. of Parliament are accused to be in it by a Letter from the D. of Q. to her Majesty last year, whereof he had a printed copy in his hand, and read parcels of it'. (Hume's report.) Fletcher returned to his charge that the origin of all the evil was the House of Lords' undue intermeddling in Scottish affairs, and once again proposed a resolution condemning the Lords and praising the Commons. Marchmont and Stair argued that the Lords' address to the Queen was a clear acknowledgement of Scottish independence and that the affair of the Plot was England's as well as Scotland's business. The Marquis of Annandale denied that the House of Commons had been motivated by any consideration for Scotland. After much rowdy discussion and some bitter personal attacks, the House returned to Fletcher's motion. The part of it concerning the House of Lords was approved, but the clause concerning the House of Commons was rejected, as savouring of interference in English legislation.

Meanwhile, Queen Anne (or rather her ministers) found reasons for indefinitely postponing any inquiry into the Scots Plot, largely under Queensberry's persuasion, who argued that further discussion of the Plot would arouse so much passion and debate that the question of succession would never be settled. Although in further meetings of the House in August the demand was again made for the production of the papers concerning the Plot, no opportunity was given for further discussion of the subject. The

result was indefinite postponement of the nomination of commissioners to discuss terms of Union. The Government thus saw
no way of mitigating the harsh anti-English implications of the
Act of Security. When the Scottish Parliament went on to pass an
Act 'prohibiting the Importing of Woollen Cloth, or Stuff, or
any Manufacture wherein there is Wooll' and allowing 'the
Exporting of Sheeps Wooll, and Woollen Yarn' in competition
with that of England, this was seen by the Government as a
deliberate affront to English susceptibilities. On 28 August this
session of Parliament concluded with the passing of a remonstrance to the Queen deploring the misbehaviour of the House of
Lords and expressing great disappointment in not having the
papers concerning the Scots Plot laid before them. The intermeddling by the Lords was again declared to be an encroachment
on the independence of the Scottish nation, and the Queen was
humbly asked 'to take such measures as may effectually prevent all
such meddling in the future'. The motion was approved, although
of course Government supporters opposed it and, as Hume
recorded, 'many of the D. of Queensberry's party were silent'.

So although the Government had got the Supply they were so
desperately seeking, in return for the 'touching' of the Act of
Security, the policy of compromise with which they had begun
the 1704 session of Parliament had not worked, and the session
ended in a Scottish mood of defiant confrontation with England
and an equivalent English response.

7. *The Climax of the Great Debate*

English reaction to the news of the passing and 'touching' of the Act of Security was delayed by excitement at the news of Marlborough's victory at Blenheim the same month (August 1704), and it was not until November that it became evident. On 20 November Lord Haversham requested a full attendance of peers at the House of Lords, which duly met in anxious mood on the 23rd to hear him give an account of the grave situation in Scotland. Haversham deplored Tweeddale's failure to resolve the succession question in Scotland and attributed it to the 'motley' nature of the administration he served as well as to a lack of zeal on the part of both English and Scottish ministers. Godolphin and those he depended on in Scotland could not have been genuine in their desire for a satisfactory compromise with Scottish feeling on the succession question. Haversham carefully refrained from putting all the blame on the Scots, and spoke more in sorrow than in anger. 'I think every man wishes these things had not been; and, in my opinion, there is no man but must say they should not have been.' He went on to diagnose what he considered the root of the trouble: 'There are two matters of all troubles: much discontent and great poverty; and whoever will now look into Scotland, will find them both in that kingdom. It is certain the nobility and gentry of Scotland are as learned and as brave as any nation in Europe can boast of; and these are generally discontented. And as to the common people, they are very numerous and very stout, but very poor. And who is the man that can answer what such a multitude, so armed, so disciplined, with such leaders, may do, especially since opportunities do so much alter men from themselves?'

There was some disagreement in the Lords about the implied attack on Godolphin, but they were in agreement that they should devote the sitting of 29 November to a full consideration of the Act of Security and its implications. Godolphin took the precaution of having the Queen herself (for the first time) attend the House both on the 29th and on 6 December when the debate was resumed. The Earl of Rochester proposed to have the Act of Security read, but Godolphin and the Whig majority opposed this as calculated to anger the Scots by an assumption of the right to review the proceedings of the Scottish Parliament. Some bitterly anti-Scottish speeches were made by opponents of the Government anxious to expatiate on the pernicious effects of the Act of Security. Godolphin defended himself by pointing to the necessity of finding money to pay the troops, adding that 'whatever ill look it might have at present, it was not without remedy'. At the end of a heated debate the Lords concluded that their best course was not to express a view of a Scottish Act but to take active steps to mitigate any adverse effects it might have.

In the course of the debate Bishop Burnet reminded the House of the political hardships under which Scotland had laboured since the Union of the Crowns and the harsh treatment meted out by the English to the Company of Scotland trading to Africa and the Indies. He also expressed surprise that no fuss had been made in England when in September 1703 the 'Act anent Peace and War' had been passed and been given the royal assent. This, he said, was 'of infinite more consequence to England than the Act of Security'. The House was now much concerned with the possibility of a Jacobite invasion from Scotland, and presented an address to the Queen asking her to fortify Newcastle and Tynemouth, repair the works at Carlisle and Hull, arm the militia of the four northern counties, and march regular troops to the Border. But the Government was not going to be panicked into such measures, and the Queen replied to this address with caution and moderation What was more immediately important, in the opinion of the majority of the House, was to take steps to make the Scottish Parliament realize that the Act of Security could only do Scotland harm. We get a running commentary on the Lords' deliberations in letters from James Johnston in London to George Baillie of Jerviswood in Scotland. Writing on 12 December Johnston tells Jerviswood what had happened:

> Yesterday the Lords orders bills to be brought in; one for empowering the Queen to name Commissioners to treat with you for an entire Union; one to declare all Scotch not settled here, or in Ireland, or in the Plantations, or that are not in the fleet or army, to be aliens. This Act is to commence from a blank day, which it's thought will be the last day of the next session of Parliament here; and it is to commence only in case neither the Union nor Succession is settled then.

Johnston goes on to tell Jerviswood that

> you may settle for the Succession upon limitations, if you please, if the Court will still venture to grant them, or you may accept of a Union. If you will do neither, you may expect all the mischief that can be done you; as it was said, you and your independence are not so great but that you must depend either on France or England, and sure they will not suffer you to depend on France, if they can help it.

On 21 December Johnston wrote:

> The Lords have sent their bill to the Commons, who are now upon it. It gives a power to the Queen to name Commissioners to treat about an absolute Unione, and makes you aliens, and forbids your cattle from the last day of the next Session, in case neither the Succession nor the Unione be settled then.

The Commons, however, decided that it was improper for the Lords to initiate legislation that included financial penalties, and instead brought in their own Bill on similar lines. This was passed and sent to the Lords on 5 February 1705. The Lords, contrary to what some expected, were perfectly happy with the Commons' measure instead of their own, and passed it at once without discussion. It received the royal assent on 14 March.

The Alien Act, as it was widely called, mentioned in its preamble the necessity of 'a nearer and more complete Union' and authorized the Queen to nominate Commissioners to treat of such a union. Then—to give the Scots time to reconsider their position —it provided that after 25 December 1705 all Scotsmen except those in the categories that Johnston had defined in his letter to Jerviswood of 12 December should be treated as aliens, and that no English horses, arms, or ammunition should be brought into Scotland nor any Scottish cattle, coals, or linen imported into England. Lockhart of Carnwath had a characteristic comment:

> This was a strange Preamble and Introduction towards an Agreement, First, to propose an Amicable Treaty to remove Grudges and Animosities betwixt the two Nations; but at the same Time threaten the Scots with their Power and Vengeance, if they did not comply with what was demanded of them: And truly all true Scotsmen looked upon it as a gross Invasion on their Liberties and Sovereignty, and an insolent Behaviour towards a free and independent People; and 'twas odd so wise a Nation as England should have been guilty of so unpolitick a Step; for they could not have proposed a more effectual Way to irritate the Scots Nation, (when I say the Scots, I exclude the Courtiers and mercenary Members of Parliament from that Category) and I look upon it as the first Rise and Cause of the general, I may say, universal Aversion, that appeared afterwards to the Union: . . .

Daniel Defoe, who was later to come to Edinburgh to propagandize for Union and to report on its prospects to Robert Harley (Speaker of the House of Commons from 1701 to 1705 and from May 1704 also Principal Secretary of State for the Northern Department), expressed an opinion not really different from Lockhart's, though Defoe was a dissenting English Whig and Lockhart a romantic Scottish Jacobite. In his *History of the Union of Great Britain*, published in 1709, Defoe listed among the 'passages' which 'tended to estrange the Nation, and as it were prepare them for a Breach, rather than for an Union', the 'Clashings of interest' with respect to the Company of Scotland trading to Africa and the Indies, the Massacre of Glencoe, 'The

Difficulties about the Succession and Limitations', the Scottish Act of Security and the English reply to it in the form of the Alien Act. This last Defoe described as 'an Act, in my opinion the most impolitic, I had almost said unjust, that ever passed that great Assembly'.

There was a sixth item in Defoe's list of factors making for estrangement between Scotland and England, 'The seizing the Ship the *Worcester*, and Execution of Captain Green, and several others'. In August 1704 the English ship the *Worcester*, wrongly believed to belong to the East India Company, entered the Firth of Forth for repairs. Shortly before, a ship belonging to the Scottish African Company, the *Annandale*, had been seized in the Thames at the instance of the East India Company on the grounds that it was infringing the East India Company's trading privileges, and the presence of the *Worcester* in the Forth provided a Scottish opportunity to get even. The Scottish Company asked the Government to arrest the *Worcester*, but no action was taken, so a group of adventurous Scots, led by Roderick Mackenzie, the secretary of the Scottish Company, boarded the *Worcester* by a ruse, and overpowered and arrested the Captain and some of the crew. Some indiscreet and not very coherent remarks made by members of the crew when plied with liquor led to a general belief that the loss of the Scottish African Company's vessel *Speedy Return*, long overdue on a voyage to the East Indies, had been the result of a deliberate act of piracy by the *Worcester*. The vessel's master, Captain Green, and fourteen of the crew were imprisoned, and finally tried on 14 March 1705 by the Court of Admiralty. They were charged with having destroyed the *Speedy Return* and her crew. Though some evidence was given suggesting that the *Worcester* had indeed attacked and destroyed a vessel and murdered its crew, there was no proof whatever that this vessel was the *Speedy Return*. But Green and all but one of the other accused were found guilty. During the long interval between the first arrest of Green and his men and their coming to trial an enormous amount of bitterness was engendered between Scotland and England. 'The Whigs make a national Jacobite business of it,' wrote Johnston to Jerviswood, 'and it will be trumped up at all the elections. They lay it entirely at Tweeddale and the New Party's door' [the New Party was what a majority of the Country Party now called themselves]. The charge was that Tweeddale and the New Party had deliberately fanned the flames in order to regain the popularity they had lost by supporting the Hanoverian succession. In fact, their failure to get an Act of Succession passed by the Scottish Parliament combined with their action over the *Worcester* case to make it difficult for Godolphin to continue with his policy of dealing with and through Tweeddale and his supporters. In the next session of Parliament, Tweeddale was replaced as Commissioner by the young Duke of Argyll.

Rumours that Green and his men would be reprieved provoked violent demonstrations by the Edinburgh mob, who threatened to break into the Tolbooth and execute the prisoners themselves. Seafield's carriage was stopped outside the Tron Church and its windows smashed: Seafield himself escaped with some difficulty into the house of a friend. On 11 April, in the face of increasing violence, Captain Green, with the mate Mader and a gunner named Simson, were brought out to execution, followed by the abusive jeers of the mob. They died courageously, protesting their innocence. Some months later the rest of the condemned members of the crew were quietly released—a sufficient indication of the injustice of executing Green and the other two, for if they were guilty the other accused men were no less so. The whole incident was in fact a savage flare-up of anti-English feeling provoked by a host of factors including memories of Darien, and served to emphasize the desperate urgency of finding a solution to the problems posed by the exacerbated relations between Scotland and England.

Meanwhile, the usual jostling for positions of power and influence took place before the opening of the next session of the Scottish Parliament on 28 June 1705. The Jerviswood correspondence clearly shows the enormous amount of intrigue that went on in the early months of that year. Argyll arrived in

Edinburgh soon after the execution of Green, having already
shown his independence by writing to Seafield asking him to
suspend the sentence. A young man in his early twenties, he had
succeeded his father in 1704 and had already distinguished himself
in Marlborough's battles on the Continent. His appointment as
Commissioner (on his own terms) signified the Government's
abandonment of Tweeddale and the New Party as means of
working out a compromise with the Scottish Parliament and a
fall back to the position of the Old or Revolution Whigs who
had consistently supported William of Orange. Argyll's relative,
the third Earl of Loudoun, a strong advocate of Union, became
joint Secretary for Scotland with the Marquis of Annandale.
Queensberry was re-instated as Lord Privy Seal. Adam Cockburn
of Ormiston, a rigid Presbyterian and old-fashioned Revolution
Whig, became Lord Justice-Clerk. Seafield retained his office as
Chancellor. Sir James Murray of Philipaugh was Clerk Register.

The three parties active in the new session of Parliament were
the Court Party, supporters of the Government, consisting now
mostly of Whig Ministers; the Country Party, now calling itself
the New Party; and the Cavaliers, mostly Jacobites and Episcopalians. The New Party, who refused to go along with the
Cavaliers whom they considered to have deserted them in 1704,
and who at the same time remained independent of the Court,
were widely known as the 'Squadrone Volante'. They were
essentially an opportunist group, strongly nationalist in feeling
and formally standing for the Hanoverian Succession with
limitations. Sir John Clerk of Penicuik, who was to be appointed
one of the commissioners for the Union, gave a somewhat
hostile report of the Squadrone in his *Memoirs*:

> These consisted of about fifteen Lords and Gentlemen, all Whigs in
> their principles, but who herded together, and kept little or no
> communication with the Duke of Queensberry and his Friends. They
> were for opposing every thing which they durst oppose, but to keep
> firmly in their view the succession of the Crown in the House of
> Hanover. They pretended to be great Patriots and to stand up chiefly
> in defence of the rights and privileges of the subjects, in a word, the

publick good and the liberty of the subjects were still in their mouths, but in their Hearts they were known to have Court preferments and places in the chiefest degree of veneration. These were the springs and motives of all their Actions, which appeared in a hundred instances thereafter. However, by the bye, I must say that such a Squadrone Volante in any Parliament seems always to be a happy means in the hand of Providence to keep the several members of an Administration in their duty, for people in great power seldom fail to take more upon them than falls to their share.

The chiefs of the Squadrone Lords were the Dukes of Montrose and Roxburgh, the Earls of Rothess and Hadington, all these young men of about 24 years of Age; but the chief of all, at least a man under whose name they principally voted, was the Marquis of Tweedale, a very good Man, but not perfectly qualified for Court intrigues.

Fletcher of Saltoun was the outstanding member of the Squadrone when he worked with it; but his position was essentially that of an independent nationalist.

Seafield, Loudoun, Annandale and the others entrusted with putting the Government view, did not find the picture easy to discern, and spent much time drafting the Queen's letter. 'I know the succession is most desirable,' wrote Seafield to Godolphin on 8 June, 'bot I am verie afraid it will not succeed at this time, and manie of her Majesties most faithful servants and who heartilie wish the setelment of the succession are of this opinion, and, if it fails, it will be a praejudice to it, and I am affraid give great strenthe and advantage to the opposing pairtie, whereas that of a treatie seems more probable to succeed ...' Writing again on 30 June, he reported that Parliament had met on the 28th but because of the absence of several members it had been adjourned until 3 July. 'Till then the opposing pairtie seems to be devided. Thos laitlie turned out seems to be for limitations, others are for a treatie, and a great manie against both. I am onlie affraid that they join in some previus resolve; if not, it is probable either the limitations or the treatie will carie, bot, had the Old and Neu parties joined, it would have done weal, bot that is nou past.'

On 3 July the Queen's letter was read:

In your last Meeting, We Recommended to you with the greatest Earnestness the Settling of the Succession of that Our Ancient Kingdom in the Protestant Line. And Several things having since happened, which shews the great Inconveniency of the Matter's continuing in suspense, We cannot but at present most seriously Renew the Recommendations of this Settlement, as being convinced of the growing Necessity thereof, both for the Preservation of the Protestant Religion, and the Peace and Safety of all Our Dominions; And for defeating the Designs and Attempts of all Our Enemies. And to prevent any Objection to the said Settlement, that can be suggested from the Views or Fears of future Inconveniences that may happen to that Our Kingdom from thence; We shall be ready to give the Royal Assent to such Provisions and Restrictions as shall be found necessary and Reasonable in such a Case: And therefore We must still leave it upon you as most necessary for all the ends above mentioned, That you go to the Settlement of the Succession before al other Business.

We are fully Satisfied (and doubt not but you are) That great Benefit would arise to all Our Subjects, by an Union of Scotland and England, and that nothing will Contribute more to the Composing of Differences, and extinguishing the Heats that are unhappily raised and fomented by the Enemies of both Nations, than the promoting of every thing that Tends to procuring the same. Therefore we earnestly Recommend to you to pass an Act for a Commission to set a Treaty on Foot between the Kingdoms, as Our Parliament of England has done, for effectuating what is so desirable, and for such other Matters and Things as may be Judged proper for Our Honour, and the Good and Advantage of both Kingdoms for ever.

The letter also made an appeal for the grant of Supplies, those already granted having come to an end. Argyll, the new Commissioner, in his speech gave a succinct resumé of the Queen's letter, and Seafield then echoed these sentiments, adding: 'It is Unquestionably the Interest of both Nations, that they were more closely United, and that there were an entire Communication of Advantages and Privileges, and that they both had the same

Interest, which would make this Island secure at Home, and Formidable Abroad.'

At first it appeared that little had changed from the previous year's session. On 17 July the Duke of Hamilton was on his feet with his by now familiar resolution: 'That this Parliament will not proceed to the Nomination of a Successor, till we have had a previous Treaty with England, in relation to our Commerce, and other Concerns with that Nation. And further, it is resolved, that this Parliament will proceed to make such Limitations and Conditions of Government, for the Rectification of our Constitution, as may secure the Liberty, Religion and Independency of this Kingdom, before they proceed to the said Nomination.' Lord Belhaven then made a very patriotic speech full of historical references. He referred to the death of Alexander III and the controversy over the succession that followed. 'The King of England gave us a King: What was the Consequence of that? Both of us paid very dear for it ... The other time ... that we groaned under English bondage, was by Cromwel.' He talked of Bruce and James I of Scotland and went on to plead for unity. 'Therefore, if we be United, and keep our Hold, and make no unreasonable Demand either of Limitations from the Queen, or Conditions from England, but meerly such as the Necessity of this Nation requires, I hope, by the Blessing of God upon our Just Endeavours, and the Cordial Support of our Most Excellent Sovereign, That we shall have all our Desires granted, and a good Understanding betwixt the two Nations promoted ... Therefore I am for the Resolve, and for beginning with the Limitations.' Belhaven's speech made a great impression, and a resolution to approve it was carried.

Seafield reported mournfully to Godolphin on the 18th that Hamilton's resolution had been carried by a majority of 43 (in spite of members of the Squadrone, apart from Belhaven, voting against it). He had consulted with the Commissioner and others 'and wee all agreed that there remains nothing now to be done concerning the succession in this session of Parliament, and that wee ought to endeavour to have ane act for a treatty in such terms as that wee might hope to have some success. So wee are to try what influence wee can have upon the members of Parliament for obtaining ane act for a treatty, leaving the nomination to the Queen, and, if we cannot prevail in that, to joyn that there will be a good nomination. If this cannot carry, wee will be necessitat to bring the session to a close as soon as wee can.'

After the House had spent some time discussing financial and commercial matters, the Earl of Mar on 20 July presented a draft of a treaty with England which provided that the appointment of officers of state should be subject to the consent of Parliament. The Government put up the Marquis of Lothian, an active unionist, to propose their version of an Act of Union. After two sittings in which the House returned to commercial matters, Lothian pressed for a first reading of his Act. Seafield reported to Godolphin on 1 August on what happened then:

> Yesterday wee recommended it to my Lord Lothean to propose the giving the act for a treatty a first reading. Att first, wee mett with nothing but high and studied speeches complaining of the English act of treatty, and that it was inconsistant with our soveraignety and independancy to treat until the menaceing clausses in the English act were recinded. It was said, on the other hand, if there was anything hard or severe upon us in that act, the only way to obtain redress was to treat, and it was not to be doubted, if this method was followed, but by her Ma^{ts} interposition and assistance, the two nations might be brought to a good correspondence and all grounds of difference removed.

Seafield went on to tell Godolphin of the arguments he had used in his own speech: he had protested his concern for the honour of Scotland yet 'could never be for a separate king or a separation from England so long as there was any possibility of getting our differences removed'. He continued:

> My reasons for conjoining with England on good termes were these: that the kingdome of England is a Protestant kingdome and that, therefore, the joyneing with them was a security for our religion. 2°, England has trade and other advantages to give us, which no other

kingdome could affoord; 3°/, England has freedome and liberty, and that the joyning with it was the best way to secure that to us; and 4°/, that I saw no other method for secureing our peace, the two kingdomes being in the same island, and forreign assistance was both dangerous to ourselves and England and that, therefor, I was for a treatty.

After this, severall others having spoke to the same purpose, the vote was near being stated to give the act of treatty a first reading or approve of the resolve presented by Mr. Fletcher of Saltoun and the addition offered by the Duke of Hamiltone (herewith sent), but they being sensible that wee could carry this, there was a new debate upon limitations and rectifying our constitutione before entering upon a treatty. Wee said that, if limitations were offered in order to the setleing of the succession promptly, and, if the resolve concerning a treatty were laid aside, wee were willing to enter upon them, but limitations without setling the succession would both postpone the succession and treatty and ruine the monarchy, and that, therfor, wee could never aggree to limitations but in ane Act of Setlement. Att last, the vote was stated, 'proceed to limitations or to the act of treatty,' and, the Cavaleer and New Party having fully conjoyned, it was caryed by a majority of three votes only to proceed to limitations. If two or three off our friends had been in the House that were absent, it had come to my casting vote and I would have given it with all my heart for a treatty . . . The Comm^r having called severalls of the Servants together this day, wee all agreed in opinion that wee should yet try if wee can gain a majority to be for a treatty, and that, in order to have time, wee may proceed to some acts of trade and limitations, and if this can result in obtaining ane act of treatty and a supply, it is well, but, if not, we must give it over for this time, . . . I have seen this day some of both the parties that joyned against us, and I have spoke very plainly to them, particularly to the Earles of Roxburgh and Belhaven, and I beleeve I have disobligded both them and their friends with my plainness. I have also done what I could to perswade Duke Hamiltone to be for the treatty, and I had very good hopes till yesterday. But I am afraid that he is now gone on so farr that it will be difficult to obtain his concurrance.

The resolution by Fletcher of Saltoun to which Seafield refers had stated that 'notwithstanding the unneighbourly and injurious useage receaved by ane act lately past in the Parliament of England' the Scottish Parliament was still willing 'in order to a good understanding between the two nations' to enter into a treaty with England, but that it was inconsistent with the honour and interest of 'this independent kingdome to make any act or appoint Commissioners for that same end' until the English Parliament had made such a proposal 'in a more neighbourly and friendly manner'. Hamilton's motion was that Parliament 'proceed to the necessary Acts for regulating our Trade, the Rectification of our present Constitution, and the Limitations in the terms of the first Resolve'.

Queensberry, Lord Privy Seal, had arrived in Edinburgh on 23 July and proceeded to take charge of the Government's strategy. But what were they to do? The Government supporters were faced by a fluctuating opposition which, while in the majority, could not be counted on to act in unison. The Cavaliers' main object was to put off the succession question by an insistence on the kind of limitations which they knew would be unacceptable to the Government. The Squadrone Volante agreed with the Cavaliers in wanting limitations before a treaty but were willing to grant the required legislation about the succession and to proceed with a treaty if they could have what they considered to be realistic limitations. When the Earl of Glasgow asked what limitations the Opposition required and went on to inquire if they did or did not want to name the successor, Hamilton shouted loudly 'No!' But a majority in the House would have been prepared to name the successor if satisfactory limitations were granted.

On 5 August Seafield wrote to Godolphin that little had occurred since his last letter except an attempt by the Opposition 'to carie a resolve for finishing acts necessarie for regulating our export and import and for limitations praevious to ane act of treatie', and that the Government had been obliged to agree to four days' meetings for trade and four for limitations before either a treaty or the question of supply could be considered. By agreeing to this, he felt, 'wee may at last carie the act for a treatie and a supplie'. He added that the New Party, or at least some of them, agreed that 'if limitations on the successor be voted, tho not past, they will then be for the treatie'.

The meetings on trade discussed an Act for encouraging herring fishing and then, on 9 August, proceeded to consider an Act for appointing a Council of Trade. On the 10th there was hot debate as to whether the Queen or Parliament should have the right to nominate the Councillors of Trade, and it was carried that Parliament should have the nomination. On 14 August the Earl of Marchmont, supported by Hamilton, Fletcher and Belhaven, moved that the Estates of Parliament should choose seven councillors each for the Council of Trade, by ballot, but after argument on the legality of this procedure the matter was dropped.

The House then proceeded to debate and to pass a number of measures none of which received the royal assent. These included an Act providing that, in case of the Queen's decease without heirs of her body, nomination of officers of State should be by Parliament; an Act for Triennial Parliaments; and an Act appointing Scots ambassadors. The Act for choosing Officers of State originally specified that the choice was to be made not by the King in Parliament but by Parliament alone, but the Government proposed a clause changing this to 'the King, with Consent of Parliament' and this was carried.

Lockhart, noting that none of these Acts received the royal assent 'though the Court promised it often to many of the Members', saw their passage as part of 'wheedling' over members of the Opposition to accept an Act of Treaty. These members, he added, thought they had achieved something real by these limitations and never imagined that 'the Treaty would terminate as it did'. He continued:

But Mr: Fletcher of Salton having, in a long Discourse, set forth the deplorable State to which the Nation was reduced, by being subjected to English Councils and Measures, while one and the same Person was King of both Kingdoms, did conclude, these above-mentioned Acts of Limitation were not sufficient; and therefore presented a Scheme of Limitations, which he proposed should be ingrossed into an Act.

These were exactly the same twelve limitations that Fletcher had presented in 1703, but this time he argued that they should be adopted not by Act of Parliament but by Claim of Right; but once again he was unable to convince the House. Seafield wrote about all this to Godolphin on 18 August, declaring that Fletcher's limitations really meant the establishment of a republic after the Queen's death. As for a Claim of Right, he had argued that 'no clame of right could be setled unless the successor were declared, and, if that were to be done, it behoved to be by ane Act of Settlement, and her Ma^{ts} consent to that Act is absolutely necessary, for the Estates, without her Ma^{ts} consent, cannot setle the successor'.

The Earl of Mar's motion for a Treaty of Union came up again on 25 August, and this gave members an opportunity to voice their anger about the Alien Act. As Hume recorded in his Diary: 'Salton, Belhaven, and in end, the Dukes of Ham. and Athol spoke against Treating till the Injurious Act of Parliament in England were rescinded.' Fletcher 'represented the scurrilous and haughty Procedure of the English in this Affair; and exhorted them to resent this Treatment, as became Scotsmen, by throwing the Motion of a Treaty, until it were proposed in more civil and equal Terms, out of the House with Indignation'. But the House rejected Fletcher's motion, and called for the reading of both Mar's draft and the English Act, which was done. Lockhart can speak for what now became the strategy of the Opposition:

> The Cavaliers and Country Parties observing that there was a great Inclination in the House to set a Treaty on Foot, thought it improper to oppose it any longer, in general Terms; and therefore resolved to endeavour to clog the Commission with such Restrictions and Povisions, as should retard the Treaty's taking Effect; and for that End, the D. of Hamilton presented a Clause to be added to the Act, in these Terms: *viz.* 'That the Union to be treated on, should no Ways derogate from any fundamental Laws, ancient Privileges, Offices, Rights, Liberties, and Dignities of this Nation.' This the

Court vigorously opposed, seeing it secluded them from treating on an entire or incorporating Union; of which the abolishing of our Parliaments, and Subversion of our Constitution, was a necessary Consequence.

Lockhart saw the kind of incorporating Union desired by the Government as designed to 'rivet the Scots in perpetual slavery' to England; while he maintained that Queensberry and the Revolution Whigs supported it out of fear that if it were not abolished a Scottish Parliament, even under a federal union, 'might take them to task, and punish them as they deserv'd'.

Arguments both passionate and subtle were put forward in support of the clause proposed by Hamilton. It was argued that it did not imply a mistrust of the Queen herself, since 'she was not in a Capacity to know the Interest and Circumstances of Scotland, so well as that of England', and that England could not take it amiss 'seeing they themselves had, before they advised with us, restricted their own Commissioners from treating on any Alteration of the Church Government of that Kingdom'. But the main argument, most eloquently voiced, was that 'we were a free, independent People; and had a Power to give what Instructions, Powers, and Restrictions we pleased to our Commissioners'. The clause, however, was rejected by two votes. Lockhart's reflections on the rejection show something of the passion with which he and those who thought like him regarded the subject:

> And here I must observe, and lament the woful Fate of this Nation; for though it was well known, that the House was to be that Day upon this grand Affair, and the Court had mustered together every Individual of their Party; yet Seven or Eight of the Cavalier and Country Parties were absent, and thereby lost this Clause; which, had it passed, would have proved a mortal Stroke to the Court; they being resolved to have laid aside the Treaty of Union, and adjourned the Parliament; by which means the Nation had been free of that fatal Thraldom, to which 'tis since subjected.

(The notion that ever since the Union, and especially after the accession of George I in 1714, Scotland had been in a state of

'fatal thraldom' was much put about by Jacobites and was genuinely believed by Prince Charles Edward when he led the rising
of 1745.)

Lockhart's melodramatic view of the Government's intentions
and of the consequences of the rejection of Hamilton's clause was
not shared by a majority of the House. But the House was concerned to make clear their feeling of bitter resentment at the Alien
Act before it would give serious consideration to any proposal for
a Treaty of Union. On 28 August Fletcher returned to his argument about removing the affront to Scotland's dignity and honour
before there could be any question of considering favourably any
proposal for a treaty about Union. He put forward a draft of an
address to the Queen in the following terms:

> We your Majesties most Loyal and Faithful Subjects, the Noblemen,
> Barons and Burgesses concerned in Parliament, humbly represent to
> your Majesty, That the Act lately past in the Parliament of England,
> containing a Proposal for a Treaty of Union of the two Kingdoms,
> is made in such injurious Terms to the Honour and Interest of this
> Nation, that we who represent this Kingdom in Parliament, can no
> ways comply with it, which we have the greater regret to refuse,
> because a Treaty of Union has in this Session been recommended to
> us by your Majesty; but out of the Sense of the Duty we owe your
> Majesty, we do declare that we shall be always ready to comply with
> any such Proposal from the Parliament of England, whenever it shall
> be made in such terms as are no ways Dishonourable and Dis-
> advantageous to the Nation.

The Duke of Atholl put his finger more specifically on the
problem when he moved a clause to be added to the draft act for
a Treaty of Union saying that commissioners for Union 'shall not
go forth of this kingdom to enter into any Treaty with those to be
appointed for England, until there be an Act past by the Parliament of England rescinding that Clause in the English Act, by
which it is enacted, That the Subjects of Scotland shall be adjudged
and taken as Aliens after the 25 of December 1705'. The Government realized the strength and the representative nature of the
feeling behind this motion. But they did not feel able to accept

Atholl's clause as part of their Act, though that is what Atholl proposed. In a strong speech on 1 September he moved that 'the first part of the said Clause rescinding that part of the English Act, declaring the Subjects of Scotland to be Aliens, after the 25 December 1705, be first under Parliament's consideration'. Together with Atholl himself, this was supported by twenty-four peers, thirty-seven barons, and eighteen members for the burghs. The Government compromised. While they could not accept Atholl's clause as part of the draft Act setting up procedure for treating about Union, they agreed that it should be voted on as a resolution and presented as an address to the Queen. This was carried, on a motion to that effect by Queensberry. Seafield reported on all this to Godolphin on 3 September, pointing out that 'wee found that all the parties were lyke to unite not to treatt whilst wee were declared aliens' so 'wee found it necessary to agree that by ane address or instruction wee should so order it as the Comm^{rs} should not enter on the treatty till the clause declaring us aliens be rescinded'.

But there was much more than this in the long letter Seafield wrote to Godolphin on 3 September 1705. It was a triumphant report on progress in the matter of the Union. For on 1 September not only was the draft Act for a Treaty of Union read and approved, but on a motion, surprisingly, by Hamilton, it was carried that the Scottish Commissioners for Union should be nominated by the Queen rather than by Parliament—which meant of course that for the most part only those favouring an incorporating union would be named Commissioners. Fletcher and others protested bitterly, but Hamilton's proposal was carried (according to Hume) by about 40 votes. Lockhart reported Hamilton's astonishing move with white-hot indignation:

> This, you may be sure, was very surprizing to the Cavaliers, and
> Country Party; 'twas what they did not expect should have been
> moved that Night, and never at any Time from his Grace, who had,
> from the beginning of the Parliament to this Day, roared and ex-
> claimed against it on all Occasions; and about 12 or 15 of them ran
> out of the House in Rage and Despair, saying loud, 'twas to no

Purpose to stay any longer, since the Duke of Hamilton had deserted, and so basely betray'd them. However, those that remained, opposed it with all their Might; and a hot Debate arose upon it, wherein the Cavaliers used the very Arguments that the D. of Hamilton had often insisted on, upon this and the like Occasions. What! leave the Nomination to the Queen! No; She is, in a Manner, a Prisoner in England, and the Estates of Scotland had taught us our Duty, in a Case nearly related to this, during the Captivity of King James I. Our Queen knew none of us, but as introduced by her English Ministry, and recommended by our Inclinations to serve that Kingdom. Our Queen never had an Opportunity to know the true Interest of our Country; and though She did, yet, as She was circumstantiated, could not shew Her Regard for it; and who then so proper to nominate Scots Commissioners to treat on Scots Affairs, as a Scots Parliament?

The tone of Seafield's letter to Godolphin was of course very different. He described the course of the debate with enormous satisfaction:

The first debate, qch was proposed by the Cavaleer Party, that the Comm^rs might be restricted by the act for treating of any thing but a federall union and spoke much against ane incorporating union. Wee did, on the other hand, argue the great advantages of a treatty and the good correspondence with England and that wee thought the powers of the Comm^rs should be as large as these contained in the English act and that the Treatters might find it necessary to treatt the terms not only of an intire union but of a federall union and the adjusting of commerce betwixt the two nations, that the two Parlia^ts might have a full view of the best method of establishing a solid union and good correspondence betwixt the two kingdomes. The New Party did att first appear favourably for our opinion, but, att last, they joined with the Cavaleer Party that the Treatters should be expressly prohibited to treatt of any incorporating union, but the clause was conceaved in other words [i.e. the words of Hamilton's motion of 17 July] yet had this import. I had severall friends whom I could not intirely influence in every thing, but in this I prevailed with them and, the vote being stated, to add that clause or not, it carried in the negative, so that, with regard to the powers, the Comm^rs are in no way restricted. . . .

All that remained [following the Government's acceptance of the resolution on an address to the Queen against the Alien Act] of the act to be adjusted was the way and manner of the nomination [of the Commissioners], so I stated in the debate that it behoved either to be done by leaving it to her Ma^{ty}, as was done in the year 1670, where it was left to King Charles the Second, and the year 1700 it was left to the Queen, or it behoved to be done by the Estates of Parliament. The Duke of Hamilton called to be heard and made a very handsome speech. He said he was sorry there was so great division and animosities among us as that he was certain wee could make no good nomination in Parliament, and he had a great deal of trust and confidence in her Ma^{ty} our soveraign, and, therfor, he proposed the nomination might be left to her Ma^{ty}. With this proposall, you may be sure, wee heartily joyned. His party was surprysed, as we also the New Party, and they proposed that the determination of this might be delayed till the next sederunt, and some of the Cavaleers had pretty sharp speeches against the Duke, but he said very boldly that he had told his opinion and saw no reason to retract it, . . . Wee all acted our parts and proceeded firmly in the matter and putt it to the vote, whether the nomination should be by the Queen or by the Parliament, and it carried it should be by the Queen, and the Duke of Hamilton did vote for the Queens nomination. This wee carryed by a greater majority, because Twedale and Roxburgh did not vote in this, though most of the New Party did vote for the Parliament, and thus yor Lo^p has the history of the whole act, only that the Cavaleer and New Party shew a great inclination to have the act throwen out. However, wee proceeded to the vote, approve the act or not, and it carryed by a considerable majority, approve, and so there is now voted a plain act of treaty leaving the nomination to her Ma^{ty}, qch I am very hopefull if rightly managed, may be the foundation of a lasting settlement betwixt the two nations . . . All that remains to be done is that her Ma^{ty} effectually prevail with the English Parliament to rescind that clause in there act declaring us aliens, qch cannot doe the least prejudice to England, and, if this is refused by the English Parliament when wee have desyred it in the most discreett manner and att the same time left to her Ma^{ty} the nomination of the Comm^rs then it will be thought universally in this kingdome that the English doe intend no good correspondence with us, and I am perswaded that now yor Lo^o may have the honour of compleetting what you have been sincerely endavouring the severall years past.

The following November it was moved in the House of Lords that the Alien Act be repealed 'except the Clause that empowers her Majesty to appoint Commissioners to treat of an Union with that Kingdom [Scotland]' and shortly afterwards the Commons, on receiving this measure from the Lords, unanimously passed it. The way was now clear to an incorporating union between Scotland and England.

The question remains, why Hamilton not only supported but himself moved the resolution that the Commissioners for Union should be nominated by the Queen rather than appointed by Parliament. It seems clear that Godolphin worked hard on him to bring him round to this point of view, and there were uneasy reports of repeated conferences between him and representatives of the Government. It was known that he himself was anxious to be one of the Commissioners, and this may well have been an important factor. Sir John Clerk of Penicuik thought that Hamilton 'from that piece of independence expected the Honour of being appointed by the Queen', adding that he was disappointed in this hope since the Government had learned by experience that 'no good cou'd be expected from Commissioners who were not sincerely disposed to drop minute things for the sake of attaining what was principally in view, the good of both nations, and the settlement of the Succession to the Crown in the Protestant line, in the meantime.' An element of mystery, however, remains. Hamilton had been and would be again the eloquent and persistent leader of an Opposition which had consistently refused to consider treating about Union until specific guarantees had been given for Scottish nationhood and Scottish dignity. This meant, in the language of the day, a federal and not an incorporating Union. That he should suddenly turn round and work for a proposal that virtually ensured that an incorporating union would take place enraged his former supporters as much as it pleasantly surprised the Government. Whatever his reasons, Hamilton had seen the Government safely through. On 8 September Parliament voted an Act of Supply for seven months. On 21 September Parliament was adjourned. This third session of Queen Anne's first (and last) Scottish Parliament finally achieved what the Government had set out to do in 1703. For, with the way clear to an incorporating union, the succession question was as good as solved: with Scotland incorporated in a unified Great Britain there would no longer be any question of a separate Scottish arrangement about a successor to Queen Anne. The 'Act for a Treaty with England' received the royal assent on 21 September 1705.

8 The Commission and After

The passing by the Scottish Parliament of the Act empowering the Queen to appoint Commissioners to treat with English Commissioners about union with England was seen by the Jacobite opponents of union in melodramatic terms as the beginning of the end of Scotland. 'From this Day may we date the Commencement of Scotland's Ruine,' wrote Lockhart of Carnwath, by which he meant the inevitability of an incorporating union. 'For I may affirm, (it consisting with my certain Knowledge) that the English, knowing the Backwardness of the Scots Nation to enter into an Incorporating Union, would, if there had been but two or three Members in the Scots Commission that opposed it, been so far from pushing it as they did, that the Treaty would have been advanced no further than those others that had been set on Foot formerly.' It was certainly true that when on 27 February 1706 the Queen nominated the thirty-one Commissioners to represent the Scottish Parliament at Westminster they were found to be committed advocates of union— except for Lockhart himself, included as the nephew of Lord Wharton, the English Whig statesman and one of the English Commissioners, presumably in the hope that he would be amenable to family influence and perhaps to placate the Jacobites: Lockhart tells us that he took no part in the proceedings, but acted as an observer on behalf of his party.

The Earl of Marchmont had tried to persuade the Government to nominate Commissioners representing a fairly wide spectrum of Scottish opinion, in order that when Union was finally agreed on it would be more easily carried in the Scottish Parliament.

But the Government were not interested in discovering the range of Scottish opinion: they were interested only in making as sure as they could of an incorporating union. Sir James Stewart, the Lord Advocate, was not appointed as he was known to be against union. Argyll refused to act, on the grounds that he had promised membership to Hamilton and Hamilton had not been nominated a member. The leaders of the New Party and members of the Squadrone Volante were excluded. Neither Tweeddale, Roxburgh, Rothes, Baillie of Jerviswood nor James Johnston (who had been dismissed from the office of Lord Clerk-Register early in 1705) was nominated. And of course the fiery independent patriot Fletcher of Saltoun was excluded. Fifteen of the Commissioners nominated were Ministers, councillors or officials. The peers included Seafield and Queensberry and a dozen others; there were four judges of the Court of Session, and ten representatives of the shires and burghs. Sir John Clerk of Penicuik, who was one of those nominated, later stated in his *Memoirs* that (although he was himself a unionist) he was reluctant to serve because he had observed a 'great backwardness in the Parliament of Scotland for an union with England of any kind whatsoever' and thought that in the end nothing would be achieved. He soon discovered how wrong he was.

The English Commissioners were not nominated until 10 April. They included the Archbishops of Canterbury and York (the latter being the only anti-unionist on the English side, on ecclesiastical grounds), Godolphin, the Earl of Pembroke (Lord President of the Council), the Duke of Newcastle (Lord Privy Seal), the Dukes of Devonshire, Somerset and Bolton, the articulate and highly influential Lord Somers, Robert Harley (later Earl of Oxford), and other important Ministers and Government officials. Somers was the man really in charge, and it was his tact, persistence, moderation and tactical skill that were largely responsible for the final outcome.

Before the Commissioners met, there was a considerable amount of pressure exerted by those in favour of 'an entire and compleat union' in the form of private letters and other communications suggesting that the only alternative to such a union was war. (It was reported that Godolphin remarked that if war with Scotland was inevitable, the sooner it came the better. After Marlborough's victory at Ramillies in May, England had no more fear of France or a French-assisted Jacobite invasion and the Scottish Jacobites knew that France was in no position to assist them.) But many of the pro-union Scottish commissioners were doubtful of the wisdon of pressing for an incorporating union initially. The Earl of Stair, a passionate unionist, wrote to the Earl of Mar in January that although he himself believed in an incorporating union, the question of free trade and the succession should be taken up first, and any progress towards union should follow gradually. But Godolphin, Harley and Somers made it quite clear to their Scottish colleagues that they would insist on a complete union. 'Your friends here', wrote Mar to William Carstares, Principal of Edinburgh University and Church of Scotland leader, 'tell us plainly that they will give us no terms that are considerable for going into their succession, if any, without going into an entire union; and if we insist upon that, they will never meet with us, for they think all the notions about federal unions and forms a mere jest or chimera.'

The Commissioners met on 16 April. Sir John Clerk of Penicuik recalled the scene:

> The Commissioners of both nations met in different apartments in the Royal palace of Westminster, which commonly goes under the name of the Cockpit. There was one great Room where they all met when they were called upon to attend the Queen, or were to exchange papers, but they never met to hold conference together except once, when the number of the Scotch Representatives for the two Houses of the British Parliament came to be debated, all their transactions were reduced in writings concerted in separate apartments. When proposals or Conditions of the union were to be made by the English Commissioners, the Scots were desired to meet them in the great Room, and their proposals were given in by the Ld Chancellor [Somers], or the keeper of the great seal, who was at that time the Lord Cooper [William, first Earl Cowper], and when the

Commissioners for Scotland had any thing to propose, or had answers to be made to the Commissioners of England, these were presented by the Ld Seafield, then Chancellor for Scotland.

Sometimes the Scots Commissioners met at the Houses of the Secretaries of State for Scotland, who were then the Earls of Mar and Loudon, the first a most famous Man at the head of the Rebellion in Scotland in the year 1715. [Mar turned Jacobite some years later, after being snubbed by King George.] He was then very forward for the union and the settlement of the succession in the Protestant family of Hannover, . . .

The first general point debated by the Commissioners for Scotland amongst themselves was whether they should propose to the English a Federal union between the two nations, or an Incorporating union. The first was most favoured by the people of Scotland, but all the Scots Commissioners, to a Man, considered it ridiculous and impracticable [this is surely an exaggeration], for that in all the Federal unions there behoved to be a supreme power lodged some where, and wherever this was lodged it hencefurth became the States General, or, in our way of speaking, the Parliament of Great Britain, under the same royal power and authority as the two nations are at present. And in things of the greatest consequence to two nations, as in Councils relating to peace and war and subsidies, it was impossible that the Representatives or their suffrages in both nations cou'd be equal, but must be regulated in proportion to the power and richness of the several publick burdens or Taxations that cou'd affect them; in a word, the Scots Commissioners saw that no Union could subsist between the two nations but an incorporating perpetual one. But after all the trouble we gave ourselves to please the people of Scotland, we knew at the time that it was but losing our labour, for the English Commissioners were positively resolved to treat on no kind of union with us but what was to be incorporating and perpetual.

In the great Room above mentioned, was a long table, sufficient to hold all the Commissioners for both Kingdomes, being about 50 feet in length. At the head of the Table, under a Canopy, was placed a large chaire, ornamented with gold lace and crimsone velvet, for the Queen, when she desired to come amongst us. On her left side sat the Chancellor of Scotland, and on her right hand the keeper of the great seal, the Ld Cooper, afterwards Chancellor of England.

The Queen came amongst us three several times, once at our first meeting, to acquaint us of her intentions and ardent good wishes for our success and unanimity in this great Transaction. At about a month thereafter she came again to enquire of our success, and had most of our Minutes read to her, and for the last time to approve of what we had done.

Politely but firmly and consistently the English Commissioners insisted that nothing less than a perpetual incorporating union would do, and on 25 April Seafield informed the English Commissioners that he and his colleagues would yield on this point, provided mutual free trade and similar privileges could be guaranteed. And indeed this was the crux of the matter, from the point of view of the Scottish commissioners. They were obtaining trade privileges and the hope of consequent increased prosperity in Scotland in exchange for Scotland's Parliament. So on the 25th a provisional agreement was reached, corresponding to what were to be the first four Articles of Union. The two kingdoms of Scotland and England would be united into one kingdom under the name of Great Britain, with one monarchy and one Parliament; the succession was to be vested in the Princess Sophia and her heirs (always provided they were Protestants); and all subjects of the United Kingdom of Great Britain would have full freedom of trade and navigation both at home and in the colonies.

Subsequent discussion centred largely on financial matters. The balancing of taxation revenue and financial benefits, in such a way as to achieve a real equality in such matters between Scotland and England, involved a variety of calculations and adjustments. The Scots were to be exempted from several taxes and duties, most of which were due to expire within a few years any way, and, with equality of duties agreed to in other respects, Scotland was to be compensated for such part of their revenue as went towards paying the English debt to the tune of £398,085 10s. The sum, known as the 'Equivalent', was also to provide money to make good losses suffered by individuals through the reduction of the coin to the English standard and refunding capital and interest to the Company of Scotland trading to Africa and the Indies, on the understanding (briefly but uselessly resisted at first by the Scottish Commissioners) that the Company be dissolved as a threat to the monopoly of the East India Company.

The next significant point to be agreed was the number of Scottish members of the Parliament of Great Britain. On 7 June the English Commissioners suggested that thirty-eight would be a reasonable number. The Scots objected and wanted fifty; a joint session was held on the 12th to try and settle the matter. The problem was to determine the principle on which the number would be decided. To decide it on the basis of population— there were about one million Scotsmen to some six million Englishmen—would have meant Scotland's being allowed 85 members. But this was unrealistic, since neither country had a genuinely democratic system of election to Parliament. The English system had little to do with simple representation of numbers: as has often been pointed out, the sparsely populated county of Cornwall returned forty-four members. On the basis of taxation—the criterion most strongly urged by the English— the Scots, considering their proportion of the land tax, would be entitled to only thirteen members, one fortieth of the existing House of Commons. It was eventually agreed that Scotland should send forty-five members to the House of Commons and that the Scottish peers should elect sixteen of their number to sit in the House of Lords.

By the third week of July the Commissioners had agreed on twenty-five articles of union. These were drawn up by a special committee of four members from each side. Four copies were made, one each for the Queen, the House of Lords, the House of Commons and the Scottish Parliament. On 22 July 1706 the articles were signed and sealed by all the Commissioners except Lockhart and the Archbishop of York, and on the 23rd they proceeded from the Cockpit to St James's Palace to announce the satisfactory conclusion of their deliberations to the Queen. 'We have made the best of it we could,' wrote Mar to the Earl of Cromarty, 'and I hope the Parliament will think it for the interest of the nation, and so ratifie it, by which there would be an end put to all our divisions, and honest people would get leave to live at peace and ease, and mind their affairs and the improvement of their country—a much better employment than the politicks.'

The twenty-five articles agreed on the union of England and Scotland into the single kingdom of Great Britain with a single Parliament, with suitably agreed conjunction of the crosses of St George and St Andrew to be used as the 'ensigns armorial' of the United Kingdom; they agreed on the succession; on financial and taxation questions; on the future position of ships belonging to the Queen's subjects in Scotland; on free trade throughout the United Kingdom; on uniformity of coinage and of weights and measures; on the numbers of Scottish representatives in the new Parliament; most significantly, they agreed that the Court of Session and Court of Justiciary should remain after the Union for all time with the same authorities and privileges as they enjoyed before the Union (subject to such regulations for the better administration of justice as might later be made by the Parliament of Great Britain), and that all other Courts in Scotland should remain, but subject to alterations by the Parliament of Great Britain. It was also agreed that measures should be taken to guarantee the security of the Church of Scotland in its Presbyterian form of government (there was to be a similar Act for securing the Church of England as by law established). All existing Scottish laws, except those relating to trade, customs and excise, should continue in effect, unless they were inconsistent with the Treaty of Union; laws concerning 'public right, policy and civil government' were distinguished from those concerning private right: the former could be made uniform throughout the United Kingdom, while the latter should continue without alteration except for the evident utility of the inhabitants of Scotland. The continuance of the rights and privileges of the royal burghs in Scotland was guaranteed.

In some respects the articles agreed on were surprisingly perfunctory. No attempt was made to define the status of the new Parliament of Great Britain. The doctrine of the sovereignty of the King in Parliament was long accepted in England, but there is doubt as to whether it was ever accepted in Scotland. Did the Parliament of Great Britain assume the functions of the superseded English Parliament for the whole of the United Kingdom? This basic constitutional question does not appear even to have been raised. It is clear that in the minds of the English Commissioners at least what was to happen was simply the subsuming of the Scottish Parliament into the much larger English Parliament, in return for freedom of trade, some financial adjustments and the guaranteeing of the continuance of the Church of Scotland and the Scottish legal system. Their dismissal from the outset of the possibility of a federal union reflected this state of mind. There was no real discussion by the Commissioners (though there was in the pamphlet war that immediately broke out) of the feasibility of a federal system or the possibility of retaining a Scottish Parliament with limited regional functions while reserving other functions to the United Kingdom Parliament. As there seems little doubt that the latter is what the majority of Scots who thought about the matter at all would have preferred, this is surprising.

It was one thing for the Commisioners to agree; it was another to have their proposals accepted by the Scottish Parliament. Clerk of Penicuik tells what happened:

> The Commissioners, on their return to Scotland, fancied themselves that as they had been doing great service to their Country in the matter of the Union, so they would be acceptable to all ranks and degrees of people, but after the Articles of Union were published by order of Parliament, such comments were made upon them, by those of the adverse party, that the Mob was almost universally set against them.
>
> Under these hardships and misrepresentations the Articles of the Union were introduced into the Parliament of Scotland. The bulk of the nation seem'd altogether averse to them, nor indeed cou'd they expect a better usage, considering who they were who were determined to oppose them, for first there were a great many disoblidged Courtiers and self-conceited Men who cou'd relish nothing but what was of their own contrivance.
>
> Next were a vast many of the Episcopal persuasion, who hated the

Union meerly because of a first intention which many of the
members of Parliament had of making the presbyterian Government
and its security the basis of any Union between the two Nations, for
tho there was no express Article concerted by the Commissioners of
the Treaty to this effect, yet it had been ... agreed as the only
Expedient to bring over the ministers of the church of Scotland, to
give the Articles of the Union so much as a hearing; and, indeed, this
was all they cou'd procure at first, for as the security of the church of
England was to follow of consequence, many of the clergy of
Scotland grew jealous of their neighbouring clergy, and endeavoured
to instill notions in the Breatheren that such a security given to the
church of England was contrary to the principles of their forefathers,
who had supported the Solemn League and Covenant.

Another set of Enemies to the Union were the Jacobites, and as
these were very numerous even in the Parliament of Scotland, they
cou'd not think of embracing a system for the union of the two
kingdoms wherein succession to the Crown was to be settled on the
House of Hannover, to the perpetual exclusion of all the successors
of the late King James.

But there were more than disappointed Courtiers, Episcopalians and Jacobites who felt indignant and indeed betrayed when
they heard of the terms agreed by the Commissioners. A national
nerve had been touched, and it was widely felt that Scottish
nationhood would be permanently diminished if the proposals
were accepted. While many—perhaps the majority—had no
clear logical reasons to put forward against the proposed terms of
union, but were against them on simple emotional grounds, others
rushed into print to argue against them with every kind of
ingenuity and a high degree of passion. 'Till the printing of
these articles,' wrote Defoe in his *History of the Union*, 'the people
were generally very desirous of the Union, as that which tended
to the putting an end to all former animosities, burying the
ancient feuds between the nations, and removing the apprehen-
sions good people on both sides had justly entertained of a new
rupture. But no sooner were these articles printed and dispersed,
than it seemed as if everybody had set themselves to raise objections, form scruples, and find faults in them; the whole nation fell

into a general kind of labour, in canvassing, banding, cavailling at the conditions.' Defoe may have exaggerated the effect of the pamphlets, for there was certainly a great deal of spontaneous opposition to the proposals, but there is no doubt that their proliferation did have some effect.

The most eloquent and voluminous of all the anti-Union pamphleteers was James Hodges whose first pamphlet, *The Rights and Interest of the two British Monarchies enquired into and cleared, with respect to Union or Separation* appeared as early as 1702 but whose arguments were much quoted in 1706, when he produced his third. In high patriotic vein Hodges boasts of the 'antiquity, honour, dignity of precedency' of Scotland over England. Scotland, the most ancient kingdom of Europe and the only one never overcome by the Romans, could condescend to a federal union on the model of the Dutch States or the Swiss Cantons, but 'no argument hath ever been made use of in pleading for an incorporating union, but what is false and sophistical'. He dismissed the economic argument with fierce contempt: it would be madness for Scotsmen to barter their national independence 'for some hogsheads of sugar, indigo, and stinking tobacco of the Plantation trade'. He foresaw the most appalling consequences for an incorporating union, including godlessness and heresy, ale and bad claret at ruinous prices, destruction of trade and depopulation.

There were also pamphlets on the other side, notably by William Paterson (*An Enquiry into the Reasonableness and Consequences of an Union with Scotland*) and by that accomplished professional Daniel Defoe (*Essay at Removing National Prejudices*). The tone of the pro-Union pamphlets tended to be both reasonable and realistic. Defoe in particular was patient and good-humoured, and both he, Paterson and others on their side gently explained what they considered to be the true economic and political facts of the case, which made any solution other than an incorporating union simply not effective as a way of solving problems agreed by both sides to be grave. The implied admission that Scotland was surrendering to *force majeure* did not win many friends in Scotland to this sort of argument. But some of the Scottish defenders of an incorporating union were as passionate in tone and violent in language as those on the other side. 'Unless we be a part of each other,' exclaimed the Earl of Cromarty in a letter to Mar, 'the union will be as a blood puddin' to bind a cat—that is, till one or the other be hungry, and then the puddin' flyes. May wee be Brittains, and down goe the old ignominious names of Scotland and England. Scotland and England are names unknown in our native language [he means Gaelic]. England is a dishonourable name, imposed on Brittain by Jutland pirates and mercenaries usurping on their lords.' Clerk of Penicuik has left a vivid account of street-corner debates. 'Here you may find several persons exalting an union of confederacy, and at the same time exclaiming against that article of the treaty concerning equal duties, customs, and excises, as if there could be an union of confederacy ... without equal burdens ... Others quarrell, amongst other things, with the charges the nation will be put to in sending up sixteen Peers and forty-five Commons to the Parliament of Great Britain, and at the same time, both in words and writings, they cry out against that number as a small, dishonourable representation. Some are regretting the extream poverty of the nation and scarcity of money; yet, notwithstanding, they exclaim against the Union as a thing that will ruin us; not considering that our case is such, that 'tis scarce conceivable how any condition of life, we can fall into, can render us more miserable and poor than we are ... In a corner of the street you may see a Presbyterian minister, a Popish priest, and an Episcopal prelate, all agreeing together in their discourse against the Union, but upon quite different views and contradictory reasons.'

Clerk considered these arguments evidence of the 'triumph in our streets' of 'wilful ignorance, contradictions, and inconsistencies'. They were certainly evidence of strong if sometimes confused anti-Union feeling. And Clerk's own argument, that no measure could make them more miserable and poor than they were, throws light on the motives of many of the Scottish Commissioners who seem to have really wanted a federal union but who conceded an incorporating union because it was only on those terms that they could get the desperately needed economic advantages they felt the Union would bring. Roxburgh, writing to Jerviswood on 28 November 1705, had summed up the reasons why people would vote for Union as 'Trade with most, Hanover with some, ease and security with others, together with a generall aversion at civill discords, intollerable poverty, and the constant oppression of a bad Ministry'. Certainly among the other points that must have weighed with the Commissioners, as they were to weigh with the members of the Scottish Parliament that finally approved the Act of Union, was the real prospect of a bloody civil war between Jacobites and Presbyterians if the succession question was not soon resolved; other factors were the genuine concessions received in respect of the continued independence of the Church of Scotland and the Scottish legal system (which made the final Treaty perhaps something less than a fully 'incorporating' one) and pressures of every kind brought to bear by agents of the Government. These pressures, which do not seem to have amounted to outright bribery but in some respects fell little short of it, amounted to a highly successful exercise in political jobbery. The pressures never relaxed for a moment throughout the critical period between October 1706 and January 1707 when Scotland's last Parliament met in its final session to debate the Treaty of Union clause by clause.

9. *The End of an Auld Sang*

In February 1704 Daniel Defoe had started the most important of the many periodicals with which he was concerned, called *A Review of the State of the English Nation*, or simply the *Review*. Its main objective was to put forward propaganda for the Government. The many persuasive articles written in support of union between Scotland and England make it quite clear how central a part of the Government's policy union now was. But, although the English Ministers wanted union so desperately, it was not popular among many classes of Englishmen, and it was these Englishmen as well as the anti-union Scots whom Defoe set himself to win over in these articles. In the issue of 3 October 1706, the day when the last session of Scotland's last Parliament opened, Defoe wrote in the *Review:*

> Nothing is more plain to me, than the absolute and mutual Necessity of a Union to both Nations, and gives me some more than usual Hopes and Expectations from this present Treaty, that indeed the Necessity of Union is so obvious, that no Man that wishes well to both Nations, but must be convinc'd of this, which I lay down as the Foundation of my Discourse, WE CANNOT BE WITHOUT IT.

Union, he argued, was the only way to peace and prosperity; the alternatives were 'a Union or a War'. In his eagerness to persuade his readers, Defoe broke into verse:

> Tis Peace and Union, make a Nation thrive,
> Give Laws their Birth, and keep those Laws alive;
> Union's the Nation's Life, and Peace the Soul,
> Union preserves the Parts, and Peace the whole; ...

No Nation can our Happiness invade,
Union our Hearts secures, and Peace our Trade; . . .
Union's your living Spring, of Means and Ways,
And Peace an unexhausted Fund of Praise; . . .

In subsequent issues Defoe brought out argument after argument
to persuade his readers that Englishmen would benefit from the
Union at least as much as Scotsmen. 'The Advantages are infinite,
unaccountable, and as Times go, incredible on both sides,' he
wrote on 10 October; 'but to say on which side the greatest, I
will not undertake to determine.' Only enemies of peace,
ignorant and misinformed railers, narrow fanatics and mischief-
makers oppose the Union:

> To the Scots they cry out, that the English will enslave them,
> that the English want a Union and they do not; that the English will
> make a meer conquer'd Kingdom of them and the like.
> To the English, they cry out of the Church being betray'd, sunk,
> and endanger'd by the Encroachments of the Kirk, and by the
> growing power of Presbytery; that their Commons in our House of
> Commons, and their Lords in our House of Lords, will always be
> ready to vote against the Church, till at last they vote Her quit out
> of Doors, and so by Consequence over-run the Nation.
> To the Scots they cry out, the English will over-run their
> establish'd Church, debauch their great Ones, and at last give up
> their Kirk to the Destroyer, whose Courtesie they have so severely
> experienc'd.

In later issues, in the face of growing anti-Union agitation in
Scotland (which he faithfully reports), Defoe addresses himself
more specifically to the Scottish objectors. He takes up one by one
the points made by Hodges and other anti-Union pamphleteers,
and, with an air of great fairness and patience, argues that that
all arose from misunderstanding or prejudice. In issue after
issue he deals with point after point, so that the modern reader
who wants to know precisely what the arguments were that were
raised against the Union in Scotland cannot do better than read
through the issues of *Review* in November and December 1706.

Defoe was to sum up his arguments in favour of Union in his Dedication to Queen Anne of his *History of the Union:*

> ... whatever Loss some may alleadge Scotland suffers in this Union, in matters of Commerce, in removing her Parliament, in lessening the Conflux of her Nobility and Gentry to Edinburgh, in Taxes, and in carrying away her People, Things which Time may Remedy and Repay her for with Interest; Yet this the most prejudic'd Man in Scotland *must acknowledge they have an Exchange*, and which *if they know how to value it*, is worth all they have paid, or can pay for it; I mean Liberty, in its due and best Extent, Religious and Civil.
>
> Those who complain of this Union in the little Articles of Commerce, and on Pretence of Inequalities, in which they never fail to redress in Parliament, as often as they apply themselves for it— should do well to look back upon the Days of Cruelty and Persecution, when the Goals [sic] were filled with their Citizens, and the Places of Execution covered with the Blood of their Ministers, when their Church was trampled under Foot, and they had no Liberty to worship GOD according to their Consciences: Even in the Felicity of a Revolution Establishment they had no Security, that these Times should not return upon them—; But by the Union, they see themselves unalterably established, their Church-Government made a Fundamental of the Constitution, and the very Church of England engaged to preserve it intire ...
>
> ... The Interests of Popery, Tyranny, French Usurpations and Spurious Succession received a mortal stab by this Union ...

It is worth keeping these arguments of Defoe in mind when we turn to the proceedings of the Scots Parliament, for in discussing these we shall be involved almost wholly in the arguments and the rhetoric of the anti-unionists and the postures they assumed in fighting what increasingly came to be seen as a losing battle against what they considered to be the loss of Scotland's nationhood.

When the session of Parliament opened on 3 October 1706, with Queensberry again as Commissioner and Seafield as Chancellor, the Queen's letter was read:

> The Union has been long Desired by both Nations, and We shall Esteem it as the greatest Glory of Our Reign to have it now Per-

fected, being fully perswaded, That it must prove the greatest Happiness of our People.

An intire and perfect Union will be the solid Foundation of lasting Peace; It will secure your Religion, Liberty and Property, remove the Animosities amongst Your Selves, and the Jealousies and Differences betwixt Our Two Kingdoms: It must increase Your Strength, Riches and Trade, and by this Union the whole Island being joyned in Affection and free from all Apprehension of different Interests, will be enabled to Resist all its Enemies, support the Protestant interest every where, and maintain the Liberties of Europe.

The letter went on to renew assurances that 'the Government of the Church, as by Law Established in Scotland' would be maintained. Queensberry then spoke, commending the terms agreed on by the Commisioners for Union as just and reasonable. He was followed by Seafield, who found them 'just, honourable and advantageous' and commended them with great force. He concluded:

Since we have now the Opportunity of Establishing for Our Selves and Our Posterity, this union with England, all that concerns Our Religion and Liberties, together with the most valuable Privileges of Trade; I am hopeful that You will proceed to the Consideration of the Articles of Treaty, in such manner as shall bring it to the desired Conclusion, and it cannot but tend to the lasting Honour of this Session of Parliament to have so happily finished this most Important and Weighty Matter.

After the reading of the Queen's letter and the speeches by Queensberry and Seafield, the Articles of Union agreed on by the Commissioners were read and ordered to be printed, with copies to be delivered to the Members of Parliament. This was done on 12 October, when the Articles of Union were read a second time and it was agreed (as the official minutes record) 'That the Parliament should proceed to the Consideration of the said Articles of Union the next Sederunt'. However, on 15 October, the Duke of Hamilton, the Duke of Atholl, Lord Belhaven, Fletcher of Saltoun and Lord Balmerino questioned the accuracy of this part of the minutes and this precipitated a long debate. According to Lockhart, many opposed a consideration of the Articles of Union at this time 'as too hasty a Procedure in so momentous an Affair, and crav'd Liberty now they had seen the Articles, to consider and advise with their Constituents concerning them, from whence arose a hot Debate, whether or not the Parliament without Particular Instructions from their Constituents, could alter the Constitution of the Government'. It was argued, against the Government view that 'the Members had ample Commissions, to do all things for the Good of the Country', that everybody knew that when this Parliament was originally chosen there was no idea of Union in view, 'besides it was so long ago, that it was not strange the Barons, Freeholders, and Burghs expected their Representatives should advise with them; and since they were not allow'd to have a new Election, That thus their Sense of this Weighty Affair might be known in Parliament'. In the end it was agreed that the minutes were correct and that Parliament should therefore proceed to consider the Articles of Union. Lord Belhaven proposed that they should delay discussion for a week, but eventually it was carried by sixty-six votes that they should proceed to the First Articles. On 17 October Articles II to VIII were read, and on the 19th Articles IX to XV.

Meanwhile, the Articles of Union having been published on the 12th and so now generally known in detail, there was great popular clamour against them. Lockhart described this with relish:

> During this Time, the Nation's Aversion to the Union increased; the Parliament Close, and the outer Parliament House, were crowded every Day when the Parliament was met, with an infinite Number of People, all exclaiming against the Union, and speaking very free Language concerning the Promoters of it. The Commissioner, as he passed along the Street, was cursed and reviled to his Face, and the Duke of Hamilton huzza'd and convey'd every Night, with a great Number of Apprentices and younger Sort of People, from the Parliament House to the Abbey, exhorting him to stand by the

Country and assuring him of his being supported. And upon the
Twenty Third of Octob. above Three or Four Hundred of them
being thus employ'd, did, as soon as they left his Grace, hasten in a
Body to the House of Sir Pat. Johnson (their late darling Provost, one
of the Commissioners of the Treaty, a great Promoter of the Union,
in Parliament, where he sat as one of the Representatives of the
Town of Edinburgh) threw Stones at his Windows, broke open his
Doors, and search'd his House for him, but he having narrowly made
his Escape, prevented his being torn in a Thousand Pieces. From
thence the Mob, which was encreas'd to a great Number, went
thro' the Streets, threatning Destruction to all the Promoters of the
Union, and continu'd for four or five Hours in this Temper; till
about three next Morning, a strong Detachment of Foot Guards was
sent to secure the Gate call'd the Netherbow Port, and keep Guard
in the Parliament Close. 'Tis not to be express'd how great the Con-
sternation was that seiz'd the Courtiers on this Occasion: Formerly
they did, or pretended not to believe the Disposition of the People
against the Union; but now they were thoroughly convinc'd of it,
and terribly affraid of their Lives. This Passage making it evident
that the Union was cramm'd down Scotland's throat.

On the other side, Defoe reported from Edinburgh to Robert
Harley on 24 October:

The first night [22 October] they Onely Threatned hard and
follow'd their Patron D. Hamilton's Chair with Huzzas from the
Parliament house quite thro' the City—They Came up again
Hallowing in the Dark, Threw some stones at the Guard, broke a
few windows and the like, and so it Ended . . .

[On the 23rd] Duke of Hamilton Came from the House in his
Chair as Usuall and Instead of Goeing Down the City to his Lodgings
Went up the High street *as was said* to Visit the D of Athol.

This whether Design'd by the D. as Most think or No, but if not
was Exactly calculated to being the Tumult—For the Mob in a Vast
Crowd attending him thither waited at the Door—and as those
people did not Come there to be Idle, The Duke Could have Done
Nothing more Directly to point Out their business, The Late Ld
Provost Sir Pat. Johnston liveing just upon the spot.

Defoe goes on to tell in great detail how the mob attacked

Sir Patrick Johnston's house and how later that evening he
'heard a Great Noise and looking Out Saw a Terrible Multitude
Come up the High street with A Drum at the head of Them
shouting and swearing and Cryeing Out all scotland would stand
together, No Union, No Union, English Dogs, and the like'.
He ends the letter by reporting that 'Two Regiments of Foot are
sent for to quarter in the City and I hope, as before, this Mob will
like Our Tackers be a Meer plott to Hasten what They Design'd
to prevent'. On 29 October he reported:

> There is an Entire Harmony in This Country Consisting in
> Universall Discords. The Church men in perticular are goeing Mad.
> The parsons are out of their wits and those who at first were brought
> Over, and pardon me Some of them My Converts, their Country
> brethren being now Come in are all Gone back and to be brought
> Over by no perswasion.

The General Assembly was not in session, but the Commission
of the General Assembly had already appointed 18 October to be
a day of prayer in the light of 'the great and weighty affairs now
in agitation'; on the 22nd they sent out a circular letter recommending every presbytery to appoint a day for 'solemn publick
prayer, fasting, and humiliation'. A service held at Edinburgh on
the 31st was, diplomatically, attended by the Commissioner and
other members of the Government. This helped to produce a
calmer atmosphere, as did the moderate attitude of Principal
Carstares, but many Presbyterian ministers remained apprehensive
about the effects of Union: they objected to the application of the
Sacramental Test in England to Scotsmen in communion with the
Church of Scotland, since this would make such Scotsmen
ineligible for office in England, and argued that the communion of
the Church of Scotland should be as effective for a Scotsmen
seeking office in England as the communion of the Church of
England would be for an Englishman. This objection was voiced
in Parliament by Hamilton on 30 October, when he protested
against 'The Sacramental Test, which made an inequality,
whereby Scotsmen are barred from imployments in England,

but Englishmen are not barred from imployments in Scotland' (Hume's report). The Government could not possibly concede the Scottish claim, however logical, that in a United Kingdom with two national churches a Church of Scotland test should be as valid for seekers of office south of the Border as north of it. But they were forced to concede that the only valid religious test in Scotland should be the Church of Scotland's Confession of Faith. The Act for Securing the Protestant Religion and Presbyterian Church Government was passed on 12 November, in spite of an objection by Lord Belhaven which was supported by twenty-three others, including Hamilton, Atholl and Fletcher, that it was inadequate. This Act, subsequently embodied in the Treaty of Union, though it did not meet all the demands of Presbyterian ministers, sufficed to procure sufficient approval for Union from the Church of Scotland. It stated specifically that the 'Government of the Church by Kirk-sessions, Presbyteries, Provincial Synods, and General Assemblies . . . shall be the only Government of the Church within the Kingdom of Scotland' and went on to provide 'That the Universities and Colleges of St Andrews, Glasgow, Aberdeen, and Edinburgh, as now Established by Law, shall continue within this Kingdom for ever. And that, in all Time coming, no Professors, Principals, Regents, Masters, or others bearing Office in any University, College or School within this Kingdom, be capable, or be admitted or allowed to continue in the Exercise of their said Functions', unless 'before, or at their Admissions, they do and shall acknowledge and profess, and shall subscribe to the [Church of Scotland] Confession of Faith, as the Confession of their Faith, and that they will practise and conform themselves to the worship presently in use in this Church, and submit themselves to the Government and Discipline thereof'. The Act also 'expressly Declares and Statutes, that None of the Subjects of this Kingdom shall be liable to, but all and every one of them for ever free of any Oath, Test, or Subscription within this Kingdom, contrary to, or inconsistent with the foresaid True Protestant Religion, and Presbyterian Church Government, Worship and Discipline, as above Established'. Without such a charter of liberty for the Church of Scotland (which to modern eyes seems in some respects—the clause relating to education for example—intolerably restrictive) the Treaty of Union could never have been passed. Even so, many individual ministers of the Church of Scotland remained bitterly opposed to it.

Meanwhile, Parliament was proceeding with the Treaty of Union clause by clause, against a background of rioting in Edinburgh and elsewhere. On 22 October the Duke of Atholl moved that 'before the Parliament agreed to the Union, the Parliament of England refound the losses of the Africa Company', but no action was taken. Parliament went on to Article XVIII, concerning trade, customs and excise. Discussion of Article XVIII continued on the 23rd, when a variety of motions were introduced. Finally, 'after a long debate and candles lighted' (Hume) the debate was adjourned until the 25th. But in fact the 25th was largely taken up with a report on and discussion of the riots of the 23rd. Discussion of Article XVIII continued on the 28th, with what Hume called 'rough reasoning upon it, as contrary to the Claim of Right, between the Marq. of Annandale and the E. of Stairs'. Then Articles XIX, XX and XXI were read. The next day they got to Article XXIII (relating to the sixteen representative Scottish peers), and Fletcher of Saltoun protested that the Commissioners had betrayed their trust. Harsh words were spoken; some called for Fletcher to go to the bar of the House; but in the end he said that 'if he had offended any person by what he said, he was sorry for it', and the matter was dropped. On 30 October the twenty-fifth and final Article was reached.

No article had yet been voted on. On 1 November Lord Marchmont moved that 'the parliament now proceed to the further and more Particular Consideration of the Articles of Union, in order to Approve them or not, and to begin with and Read the First Article'. Again it was objected that members should first have the opportunity to consult with their constituents. Then a number of petitions and addresses were presented by barons, freeholders and 'a great many fermorers and tennants' in

Midlothian, Linlithgow and Perth 'all against allowing of an Incorporated Union with England, and all read and Discoursed on'. The discussion about delaying the vote on Article I was dropped, and it was agreed 'that the First Article of Union should be Read, but that it should be intire next Sederunt of parliament to Debate whether or not the first Article should be concluded by Approving thereof or not'. Article I was again read on 2 November, but discussion of it was deflected for a time by the introduction of the Church issue. Stewart of Pardovan, a passionate Presbyterian, moved that Parliament should settle the Church issue before considering any of the Articles, but on a vote being taken, it was decided by 36 votes to consider the first Article.

Article I of the proposed Treaty of Union, providing for the union of the two kingdoms of Scotland and England in one kingdom by the name of Great Britain, was the single most crucial article of all: if it was passed, an incorporating union was settled. All sides recognized this, although the Lord Clerk Register, for the Government, tried to placate some of the Opposition's fears by proposing that if the other Articles of Union were not agreed by Parliament, then agreement to the first Article would be of no effect. Seton of Pitmedden made a long and eloquent speech stressing the commercial benefits of union and pouring scorn on the notion of a federal union as a mere playing with words. He cited the history of England, France and Spain as proving the benefits of incorporation. He was answered by Lord Belhaven in a high rhetorical speech which caused something of a sensation, though Seafield reported to Godolphin next day that it was 'contrived to incense the common people' and 'had no great influence in the House'. Belhaven's speech consisted largely of a series of pictures of what Scotland would become as the consequence of an incorporating union:

> I think, I see a Free and Independent Kingdom delivering up That, which all the World hath been fighting for, since the days of Nimrod; yea, that for which most of all the Empires, Kingdoms, States, Principalities and Dukedoms of Europe, are at this very time engaged in the most Bloody and Cruel Wars that ever were, to wit, A Power

to Manage their own Affairs by themselves, without the Assistance
and Counsel of any other.

I think, I see a National Church, founded upon a Rock, secured
by a Claim of Right, hedged and fenced about by the strictest and
pointedest Legal Sanction that Sovereignty could contrive, volun-
tarily descending into a Plain, upon an equal level with Jews, Papists,
Socinians, Arminians, Anabaptists, and other Sectaries, &c.

I think I see the Noble and Honourable Peerage of Scotland, whose
Valiant Predecessors led Armies against their Enemies upon their
own proper Charges and Expenses, now divested of their Followers
and Vassalages, and put upon such an Equal Foot with their Vassals,
that I think I see a petty English Excise-man receive more Homage
and Respect, than what was paid formerly to their quondam
Maccallanmores . . .

Belhaven went on to paint a picture of the degradation of the
Scottish peers, barons, burghs, judges, soldiery, tradesmen,
ploughmen, landed gentry and sailors, before rising to a climax:

But above all, My Lord, I think I see our Ancient Mother
CALEDONIA, like Caesar sitting in the midst of our Senate, Rufully
looking round about her, Covering her self with her Royal Garment,
attending the Fatal Blow, and breathing out her last with a *Et tu
quoque mi fili.*

Belhaven went on to cite the Roman hatred of parricide and to
urge that patricide, murder of one's native land, was an even more
hideous crime. The scheme for union would benefit England and
destroy Scotland, for it would maintain the English constitution
intact while subjecting the Scottish constitution to 'regulations or
annihilations'. 'Good God! what! Is this an entire surrender?'
he burst out, and asked for time to shed a silent tear. After a
pause, filled with comments and exclamations from other members,
Belhaven resumed his speech in a less emotional tone, arguing
that it was folly to agree to an incorporating union without first
discussing the provisions and moving accordingly that the
House begin with Article IV (about freedom of trade and
navigation).

The Earl of Marchmont then arose to deflate Belhaven's rhetoric. 'Behold, he dreamed, but lo! when he awoke, he found it was a dream,' was his most incisive comment. The 'long Reasoning and Debate' (as the official minutes describe the day's proceedings) lasted from eleven in the morning until eight at night, when (the 2nd being a Saturday) the House was adjourned until Monday the 4th. In the course of the day an address was handed in from 'the Barrons, Freeholders, Heretors and other Gentlemen in the Shire of Forfar' protesting against an incorporating union with England. On the 4th, before proceedings began, similar addresses were presented from Stirling and Dumbarton, the Magistrates, Town Council, Deacons of Crafts and Burgesses of Linlithgow, inhabitants of Dunkeld, and the town and parish of Dysart. Similar addresses were handed in almost daily at subsequent meetings of Parliament: to take only a few examples, they came from the shire of Fife and the burgh of Falkland on 6 November; from the merchants and traders of Glasgow [who were in fact to benefit conspicuously by the Union and many of whom acted under duress from the mob] and the barons, heritors and freeholders of Lanark on the 15th; from the Stewartry of Kirkcudbright, the parish of Crawford, the burgh of Coupar (Fife), and the Presbytery of Lanark on the 18th; the town of Paisley on the 21st; the inhabitants of the Sheriffdom of Roxburgh, the burghs of Annan and Lochmaben and the parish of Lesmahago on the 26th; the shire of Mid-Lothian on the 27th; the Presbytery of Dunblane and a great variety of parishes in Perthshire on 11 December; the shire of Berwick on 16 December; a variety of Ayrshire parishes on the 24th; the shires of Aberdeen and Kincardine and the towns of Stonehaven and Peterhead on 6 January; the town of Perth on 10 January. The handing in of all these protests—some ninety in all—was recorded without comment in the official minutes. In the House, where the addresses were piling up on the table, the Duke of Argyll proposed that they should be used for making kites.

On 4 November the Clark Register's earlier proposal making acceptance of Article I conditional on acceptance of the other articles was approved, and then debate on the article continued. All the standard arguments against union were advanced. The Marquis of Annandale offered a resolution 'That we are willing to enter into such an Union with our Neighbours of England, as shall Unite us intirely, and after the most strict manner, in all their and our Interests of Succession, Wars, Alliances and Trade, Reserving to Us the Sovereignty and Independency of Our Crown and Monarchy, and Immunities of the Kingdom, and the Constitution and Frame of our Fundamental Constitution, by our Claim of Right, and by the Laws following thereupon.' This was rejected, and eventually Article I was approved by 32 votes. All but two of the Squadrone Volante's members (who now numbered 24) voted for the Government: if the Squadrone had voted with the Opposition the article would have been defeated by twelve votes.

Before the vote was taken, the Duke of Atholl gave in a protest: 'That an Incorporating Union of the Crown and Kingdom of Scotland, with the Crown and Kingdom of England, and, that both Nations should be represented by one and the same Parliament, as contained in the Articles of the Treaty of Union, Is contrair to the Honour, Interest, Fundamental Laws and Constitution of this Kingdom, The Birth-right of the Peers, the Rights and Priviledges of the Barrons, and Burrows, and is contrair to the Claim of Right, Property and Liberty of the Subjects, and third Act of Her Majesties Parliament One thousand seven hundred and three, by which it is Declared high Treason, in any of the Subjects of this Kingdom to quarrel or endeavour by Writing, malicious and advised Speaking, or other open Act or Deed, To alter or innovat the Claim of Right or any Article thereof.' Hamilton, Annandale and eighteen other peers, together with Lockhart of Carnwath, Fletcher of Saltoun and forty-five other gentlemen 'adhered' to this protest. But it was a gesture merely: with the passing of Article I it was clear that the Government had a majority in this Parliament for the Treaty of Union as a whole, and all was over bar the shouting.

Seafield, however, still had his doubts. Reporting to Godolphin on 7 November he announced the majority of 32 votes for the first articles, and continued:

> Ther have been several addresses against the Union presented to the Parlament, bot what troubls me most is that from the Commission of the Assemblie, which declairs the Union inconsistant with ther principels, it being contrarie to the Covenant that the bishops sitt in the Parlament, bot I have not see it . . . A majoritie of a convention of borous [the influential Convention of Royal Brughs] have also addressed against it. . . . The Jacobit Partie continou to oppose it with violence. The Neu Pairtie, the E. of Marchmont and L. of Cromertie gives us al the assistance wee can desire. [He is referring to the fact that he was confident that he had now got the Squadrone on his side.] The D. of Argyle influences the M. of Lothean and his oun friends, so your Lop. sees wee have a majoritie that I hope will not fail us, . . .

Seafield's anxiety about the Church was largely removed after the debate on securing the rights of the Church of Scotland which occupied the House from 4 to 12 November, when the Act for Securing the Protestant Religion and Presbyterian Church Government was passed.

Article II (settling the succession 'to the Monarchy of the United Kingdom of Great Britain' on the Electress Sophia of Hanover and her heirs) was debated on 15 November. The Opposition, with increasing desperation, continued the struggle, with Fletcher and others renewing the old demand for limitations. Hamilton made a long speech in which he asked for a recess to provide time to address the Queen 'and to lay before Her the Condition of the Nation, and the great Aversion in many Persons to an incorporating Union with England, and to acquaint Her Majesty of the Inclinations and Willingness to settle the Succession in the Protestant Line upon Limitations'. The Government naturally strongly opposed this proposal (which, said Lockhart, 'was most disagreeable to the Courtiers, for they had heretofore been at great Pains to conceal the true State and Inclinations of the People from their Friends in England'—an

unfair charge, as Seafield's letters to Godolphin and Defoe's to
Harley show: the fact is that, provided they could get the Articles
of Union passed, the Government were not really interested in
what the people of Scotland thought of them). After what Hume
called 'long debate and sharp expressions' Hamilton moved that
they should proceed to vote on Article II. Belhaven then moved
that they should vote on whether to approve the article or address
the Queen, and it was carried that there should be a vote on the
article. Hamilton demanded further time to speak before the
vote and here was 'a great clamour for a long time' (Hume).
Another vote was taken on whether to proceed to the vote or
delay, and it was carried by 39 votes thay they should proceed to
the vote. Article II was then voted on and carried by fifty-eight
votes.

On Monday 18 November debate began on Article III (that
'the United Kingdom of Great Britain be Represented by one and
the same Parliament to be stiled the Parliament of Great Britain').
The Opposition made a determined and united effort to prevent
the disappearance of the Scottish Parliament, the Country Party,
in Lockhart's words, doing 'all that Men could do to shew what
Destruction this alone, supposing there was no more, would
bring infallibly upon the Nation'. Hamilton moved that 'the
Representatives from North Britain should have a negative in
matters essential and fundamental in the Union, and upon
incroachment, the Union be *ipso facto* dissolved', to which the
Earl of Stair replied that the proper time for considering guarantees
would be after all the articles had been gone through. Annandale
entered a protest asserting the general aversion of the nation to an
incorporating union 'as subversive of the Sovereignty, Fundamental Constitution and Claim of Right of this Kingdom, and as
threatning Ruin to this Church, as by Law establish'd' and
describing such a union as 'contrary to the Honour, Interest,
Fundamental Laws and Constitution of this Kingdom'. Fifty-
three members 'adhered' to this protest. Seton of Pitmedden made
a carefully reasoned speech in defence of the article, arguing that
the Government of Scotland was not a democracy or an aristocracy

but a limited monarchy, with the supreme court of Parliament subject to no higher authority. A United Kingdom Parliament could only preserve and could not threaten the rights of all the people. As for talk of surrender, nothing could be called a surrender which was the subject of a treaty. He quoted the Great Dutch jurist Grotius to the effect that 'the rights and privileges of two nations united, are consolidated into one by a mutual communication of them' and also on the question of the number of Scottish members in the united Parliament chosen on grounds of population and taxation. Article II was finally put to the vote and approved by 114 to 57. Once again Tweeddale, Roxburgh, Rothes, Haddington and other leading men of the Squadrone, with most of their followers, voted with the Government. And once again the list of voters in the 'No' column was headed by the Dukes of Hamilton and Atholl and included the Earl of Errol, the Earl Marischal, the Earls of Wigton, Strathmore and Galloway. The list of 'barons' in this column was headed by Lockhart of Carnwath and Fletcher of Saltoun. This was the pattern throughout the voting on the Articles of Union.

On 19 November the Chancellor reported to the House that the Commissioner had been attacked and insulted by a stone-throwing mob, and the Provost of Edinburgh was summoned and asked 'why nothing was done against them who were prisoners for the last mob'. Then the House proceeded to Article IV, about freedom of trade and navigation among 'all the Subjects of the United Kingdom of Great Britain'. Fletcher made a long speech in which he argued that, contrary to what was generally believed, free trade between Scotland and England would be positively disadvantageous to Scotland. Sir David Dalrymple replied in an equally long speech arguing the advantages of such trade. Saltoun was accused of simply trying 'to protract and delay business'. The Chancellor said that if members were not ready, he would adjourn the debate until 21 November. But the result was a foregone conclusion, and on 21 November Article IV was passed by 156 to 19.

With a United Kingdom, a single Parliament, a single monarch, and free trade between the parts of the United Kingdom agreed, all other matters were now largely technicalities. Parliament had agreed to an incorporating union. Violence in the streets— including ugly scenes in Glasgow on 8 and 9 November when, stimulated by anti-unionist preachers, the mob attacked the Provost's house and compelled the magistrates to sign an anti-union address—and addresses to the House made no impression whatever on the Government, who were only interested in the vote in the House. Article V (on the ownership of Scottish ships after the Union) was passed on 23 November after minor amendment. Article VI (a long and technical article mostly about customs) produced a great deal of discussion on 27 November and was remitted for further consideration to the committee that had already been set up to examine the calculation of the Equivalent: the object was to protect the interests of the Scottish farmer and trader from Irish competition. Article VII (on exciseable liquors) was approved on the 28th after an amendment guaranteeing that Scottish twopenny ale would never bear a higher excise duty than it bore at the moment—thus effectively disposing of one anti-union charge, that the Union would increase the price of the Scotsman's beer. English beer, being stronger and more expensive than Scots, bore a higher duty.

On 29 November the House received reports of anti-union riots in Glasgow, Dumfries and elsewhere. In Dumfries a copy of the Articles of Union had beeen publicly burned on 21 November. The House spent two days debating an appropriate proclamation and an Act (passed on the 30th) forbidding all assembly in arms during the current session of Parliament. Articles IX to XIII, all on financial matters, were passed in Hume's words, 'with very little struggle' on 3 December. But when the House came to Article XIV on 5 December the irrepressible Fletcher of Saltoun was on his feet again. This article provided that Scotland should not be charged with any other duties imposed by the English Parliament before the Union except those consented to in this Treaty, but that if the English Parliament were to impose any further customs or excise duties 'with which by virtue of this Treaty,

Scotland is to be charged equally with England' then Scotland would be liable to the same customs and excise duties as England, with some adjustments, with the proviso that no malt tax should be imposed in Scotland 'during this present war'. Fletcher proposed that malt in Scotland should be free of all duty for ever. Others proposed different lengths of time. It was eventually carried that the exemption should be for the duration of the war only. The next day Fletcher moved that 'the nation of Scotland be for ever free of all burdens, but what is aggreed to by these Articles'. In the end 'after long reasoning' (Hume) Article XIV was carried by 18 votes.

On 7 December Article XV (a very long article on finance, which included the provision of the Equivalent to be paid to Scotland) was read and the report from the Committee for examining the calculation of the Equivalent was received and discussed. Fletcher moved that 'they shall not be subject to the English debts' and a noisy debate followed. At length the first paragraph (giving the amount of the Equivalent) was put to the vote and was carried by an overwhelming majority. This time Hamilton voted with the Government, though Atholl still voted 'No', the only duke who did so on this vote. Hume says that Belhaven also voted with the Government, but the official minutes do not record his name as having voted on either side. The point of course was that if the Union, as now looked so likely, was going to take place anyway, Scotland at least ought to get its money.

On 10 December the House received the report of the committee on Article VI, dealing with importing and exporting foodstuffs. Surprisingly perhaps, passions ran high in debate on the technical financial and commercial matters involved, perhaps because they were now the only points left on which the frustrated feelings of the nationalists could vent themselves. Discussion on the Article continued until 16 December, when it was approved and Article VIII, which had also been referred to the committee, was discussed. This article was concerned largely with duties on imported salt, and considerable debate took place on the precise nature of the exceptions that should be made (to Scotland's advantage) to the principle of equal duties payable throughout the United Kingdom. The Article was discussed clause by clause and amendments to individual clauses offered and voted on between 16 and 26 December, when the Article finally passed, as amended. The House then returned to Article XV (of which only the first clause had so far been discussed and approved). This long and complicated article, dealing not only with the Equivalent but with a variety of financial and trade matters including the currency and compensation for the losses incurred by the African and Indian Company of Scotland, as well as the dissolution of the company, was finally passed, after considerable alteration and amendment, on 30 December. The vote was 112 for and 54 against, with, as usual, Hamilton, Atholl and Annandale together with Lockhart of Carnwath and Fletcher of Saltoun prominent among those who voted against the article.

The debate on Article VIII was enlivened on 17 December by an altercation between Fletcher and the Earl of Stair. Fletcher accused Stair of having said something 'in reference to the Minutes' which was not true, whereupon Stair (in Hume's account) 'desired the House to take notice of what Salton had said, otherwise he would be obliged to say What he had said was a lye. After near an hour's discourse about this, and some having moved That both should crave the House pardon, Salton craved the House pardon, but shifted craving Stair's pardon.' The Chancellor at length found a reconciling form of words, which was assented to by both Fletcher and Stair. This closed the incident, which reflected the high state of emotion on both sides and also something of the personal animosity that seemed to prevail between Fletcher and Stair throughout this session of Parliament until Stair dropped dead 'of an apoplexy' on 8 January 1707.

Article XVI (on standardizing the coinage) was read and approved on 31 December, and the House went on to read and approve ('after some Reasoning thereon') Articles XVII (on weights and measures) and XVIII. Article XVIII was an important clause guaranteeing that all laws in use in Scotland, other than

those regulating trade, customs and excise to which Scotland
would be liable under the Treaty of Union, would 'remain in the
same force as before' although alterable by the Parliament of
Great Britain. This Article also recognized a difference 'betwixt
the Laws concerning publick Right, Policy, and Civil Government, and those which concern private Right': the former
'may be made the same throughout the whole United Kingdom',
while the latter could not be altered 'except for evident utility
of the subjects within Scotland'.

On 2 January 1707 the House considered Article XIX, on the
preservation of an independent Scottish judicial system. An
amendment adding Writers to the Signet (under certain conditions) to those eligible to be Lords of Session was moved and
passed. The precise nature of the conditions under which they
could be eligible occupied two days' debate. Article XIX as
amended was approved on 3 January. Article XX (on heritable
offices) was passed after some minor amendment on 6 January,
and immediately afterwards Article XXI (on maintaining the
rights and privileges of the Royal Burghs) was passed with only
twenty-one votes against.

Article XXII (specifying that sixteen Scottish representative
peers should sit in the House of Lords and Scotland should have
forty-five representatives in the Commons) caused more controversy. Before the vote on the all-important first paragraph,
which gave the numbers, several protests against the vote were
handed in, one by the Duke of Atholl, one by the Earl of Buchan,
a third by Lockhart of Carnwath and a fourth by Walter Steuart,
member for the burgh of Linlithgow. Then the Earl of Errol
protested against any diminution that might be brought about by
any part of the Treaty of Union against his rights and privileges as
hereditary High Constable of Scotland. The Earl Marischal
followed with a protest against any derogation or prejudice to the
rights, dignities, titles and honours of himself and his successors in
their office of Grand Marischal of Scotland. Then the first
paragraph of Article XXII was voted on and approved by 113
votes to 74. Then the second paragraph of Article XXII (about

the manner of summoning Parliament and the choosing of the Scottish representatives) was read and strenuously debated before finally voted on and approved, after amendment. The Earl of Abercorn formally protested 'against the settling the representatives of Scotland for the Parliament of Great Britain after a distinct manner' because he could not 'see clearly into what may be the Consequences thereof'.

On 9 January the House debated the third clause in Article XXII allowing existing members of the English Parliament to continue after the Union as members of the Parliament of Great Britain if the Queen considered it expedient. The day's proceedings began noisily with discussion of the previous day's protests and the entering of new ones. After much 'reasoning', three votes were taken. The first was whether to vote first on a motion approving this clause or on a motion 'that the Parliament of Great-Britain shall meet and sit once in three years at least in that part of Great-Britain now called Scotland'. It was carried by 102 votes to 59 that the vote should be on approving the third clause of Article XXII. The vote on that clause was then taken, and the clause was passed by 106 votes to 54. A third vote, to approve Article XXII as a whole, was then taken, and the article was approved by 83 votes to 65—a drop in the Government's majority which perhaps indicated that some of its supporters were now so confident that they considered they need not stay for the vote.

10 January was largely taken up with debate on a motion providing that all holders of public office in Scotland should take a 'sacramental test' of loyalty to the established Church of Scotland, so long as a similar test of loyalty to the Church of England was required in England. The motion to add this provision to Article XXII was defeated by 68 votes to 62. The issue was a confused one, for it did not divide the unionists and the anti-unionists as clearly as some others. Many of the anti-unionist nationalists were Episcopalians, while others were enthusiastic Presbyterians. A sacramental test in Scotland prescribing loyalty to the Church of Scotland could be seen as an assertion of Scottish identity, but

it had other implications if considered ecclesiastically and theo-
logically rather than nationally. However, anti-unionist national
feeling brought together extreme Presbyterians and prelatist
Jacobites.

13 January was taken up with debate on the rights of Scottish
peers in the House of Lords: a motion that they had the right to
sit covered in the House of Lords was defeated by 90 votes to 51.
This was after the reading of Article XXIII, dealing with the
rights and privileges of the sixteen representative peers of Scotland.
The article guaranteed to these peers 'all Priviledges of Parliament
which the Peers of England now have, and which They or any
Peers of Great Britain shall have after the Union, and particularly
the Right of sitting upon the tryals of Peers'. (The last point was
conceded in an amendment.) It also provided that 'all Peers of
Scotland, and their successors to their Honours and Dignities,
shall from and after the Union be Peers of Great Britain'. Article
XXIII was voted on and approved: for some reason the official
minutes do not give the voting figures. Article XXIV (concerning 'One Great Seal for the United Kingdom of Great
Britain different from the Great Seal of either Kingdom' and
similar matters) was voted on and approved on the 14th, after the
House had approved a motion by the Lyon King of Arms leaving
his rank and precedency to the Queen. A further successful
amendment guaranteed that 'the Crown, Sceptre & Sword of
State, Records of Parliament, and all other Records, Rolls and
Registers whatsomever both publick and private, general and
particular, and Warrands thereof, continue to be keeped as they
are, in that part of the United Kingdom, now called Scotland'.
Article XXV, declaring void all laws and statutes of either
kingdom that were contrary to or inconsistent with the terms of
the Articles of Union, was approved the same day.

On 15 January there was some debate on whether the House
should proceed to discuss the manner of electing the representatives of Scotland to the Parliament of Great Britain, but it was
voted that this matter should be discussed after the ratification of
the complete Treaty of Union. The Act 'Ratifying, Approving and

at length Narrating the Articles of Union as Explained and Amended, and the Act for Security of the Protestant Religion and Presbyterian Church Government' were then read, and a first reading was agreed. A second reading of the Act to approve the Articles of Union took place the following day and was passed by 109 votes to 69. As usual, Hamilton, Annandale and Belhaven voted against it, as did sixteen other members of the nobility. Fletcher of Saltoun was among the thirty 'barons' who voted against: Lockhart of Carnwath could not bring himself to be present at what he knew would be a final commitment to Union. Twenty burgh representatives voted against, as opposed to thirty who voted in favour. And once again Montrose, Rothes, Roxburgh, Haddington and most other members of the Squadrone voted in favour. The Act was touched with the royal sceptre by the Commissioner immediately after the vote.

On 21 January after much discussion, and protests by Hamilton and others, an Act was passed establishing the method of electing the sixteen Scottish peers and forty-five Scottish members to sit in the Parliament of Great Britain by 84 votes to 65. This was an enabling Act, and did not provide a specific method. The method was discussed on the 22nd, when it was agreed that the representative peers should be chosen by the total number of Scottish peers by open election rather than by balloting. Discussion of the method of electing the forty-five members of the Commons went on throughout the next few days—first the thirty representatives of the shires and then the fifteen representatives of the burghs. The burghs were grouped into fifteen districts with one representative for each district. Only Edinburgh was given a representative to itself. Further details of the election of the sixteen peers were discussed on 3 February, and it was agreed that absent peers could vote by proxy and that the place of voting could be anywhere in Scotland agreed by Her Majesty.

The remaining days of this session were taken up with a variety of minor matters and in finally settling the affairs of the Company trading to Africa and the Indies. On Wednesday 19

March Queensberry, the Commissioner, made a speech concluding:

> My Lords and Gentlemen, It's a great satisfaction to the Queen that the Union is thus happily concluded in Her Reign, and I'm commanded by Her Majesty to assure you, that nothing shall be omitted on Her part, to make the whole Island feel the good Effects of it.
>
> And as I doubt not but the finishing of this great Affair is acceptable to you, so I hope you will study to promote a cordial Union with our Neighbours, for the greater Happiness and Advantage of both Kingdoms.

The Parliament of Scotland met for the last time on 25 March 1707, when Queensberry made his final speech.

> My Lords and Gentlemen,
> The Publick Business of this Session being now over, it is full time to put an end to it.
>
> I am perswaded that we and our Posterity will reap the benefit of Union of the two Kingdoms, and I doubt not, that as this Parliament has had the honour to conclude it, you will in your several Stations recommend to the People of the Nation, a grateful Sense of Her Majesties Goodness and great Care for the Welfare of her Subjects, in bringing this important Affair to Perfection, and that you will promote an universal Desire in this Kingdom to become one in Hearts and Affections, as we are inseparably joyn'd in interest with our Neighbour Nation.

The last word, however, was Seafield's. 'Now there's an end of an auld sang,' he said as he signed the exemplification of the Act and returned it to the clerk. He spoke with complacency rather than nostalgia, for though he and the Union were execrated by many in Scotland he had accomplished the mission on which he had long set his heart. Reviled in Scotland, he was hailed with enthusiasm in England on his southward progress to London in April. Berwick, Newcastle, Durham and other English towns received him triumphantly. Sir John Clerk of Penicuik, one of the Commissioners for the Union and a consistent voter in its favour in the Scottish Parliament, described in his *Memoirs* what happened after that:

On the 1 of May 1707 the Union of the two Nations, as had been agreed to, took place. That day was solemnized by her Majesty and those who had been members of both Houses of Parliament with the greatest splendour. A very numerous procession accompanied the Queen to the Cathedral church of St. Paul, at least 3 or 400 coaches. The Bishops and Peers sat in Galleries on her Majesty's right hand, and the late members of the House of Commons in England, with such as had been chosen to represent the Commons of Scotland in the first British Parliament on her left hand. I think there were not above half a dussan of the Scots commoners then in London, and amongst them I had the happiness to be present at this solemn piece of Devotion.

There was a sermon by the Bishop of London, followed by prayers of thanksgiving. 'A fine piece of Musick closed the solemnity.' Clerk continued:

On this occasion I observed a real joy and satisfaction in the Citizens of London, for they were terribly apprehensive of confusions from Scotland in case the Union had not taken place. That whole day was spent in feasting, ringing of Bells, and illuminations, and I have reason to believe that at no time Scotsmen were more acceptable to the English than on that day.

Sentiment in Scotland, however, was rather different.

10. After the Union

Desperate attempts were made in Scotland outside Parliament to prevent the passing of the Treaty of Union. The Glasgow riots of late November and early December 1706 seemed at one point to threaten actual armed rebellion, and on 30 November Parliament suspended the clause in the Act of Security which provided for the arming of the people. News of this measure provoked further rioting, with the forcible entry of rioters into the Tolbooth and the ransacking of houses for arms, but on 5 December a detachment of dragoons succeeded in arresting the leaders and bringing them to Edinburgh. A more serious threat to the Government was posed by the plan for a joint rising against the Union by the Cameronians of the south-west and the Jacobites of the North. The coming together of these traditional opponents—the extreme Covenanting Whigs and the romantic Tory Jacobites loyal to the exiled Catholic house of Stewart—indicated the desperation of the anti-Union forces as well as the common Scottish nationalism which was shared by two groups who read the history of Scotland so totally differently. Lockhart of Carnwath described the plan for 'above Seven or Eight Thousand Men well Armed' to assemble at Hamilton and march on Edinburgh, which they would have done, he says, 'had not the Duke of Hamilton, a day or two before the prefixed time of their Rendesvouz, sent Expresses privately ... thro' the whole Country, strictly requiring them to put off their Design at this Time.' As Lockhart succinctly summed it up in a marginal note, the scheme was 'Broke by the Duke of Hamilton', perhaps because he knew that English forces were assembling at Berwick.

Another scheme was then devised, which was, again in Lockhart's words, 'to invite as many of the Barons, Freeholders, and
Heritors, as could possibly be got to Edinburgh, that they might
in a Body wait upon the high Commissioner, and by a Prolocutor
intreat his Grace to lay aside the designed Union, at least grant a
Recess until they had informed the Queen of the present Temper
and Disposition of the Nation, and obtained an Order for calling
for a New Parliament to settle and provide for the Calamities
that were too likely to follow' and if this was refused by the
Commissioner then an address in these terms should be sent to the
Queen. But this too was 'Broke by the Duke of Hamilton', who
made it a condition of approving the address that those who
signed it should intimate their willingness to accept the Hanoverian
succession—a condition of course quite unacceptable to the
Jacobites. A third plan was that the anti-Union members, after
protesting against Article XXII (giving details of Scottish representation in the British Parliament) should all withdraw from the
House. This plan, says Lockhart, 'caused an universal Joy, and
great Numbers of Gentlemen and eminent Citizens flock'd
together that Morning about the Parliament House to convey the
separating Members, and assist them in case they should be
maltreated as they came from the House; but all their Hopes soon
vanished and came to nothing, for that Morning the Duke of
Hamilton pretended to be seized of the Toothach, refused to go
to the House.' Again, Lockhart noted in the margin, 'The Measure
broke by the Duke of Hamilton'.

All this went on while the final Articles of Union were being
debated in the House, where Hamilton consistently voted against
them and made some passionate patriotic anti-Union speeches.
('Shall we in Half an Hour yield what our Forefathers maintain'd
with their Lives and Fortunes for many ages; are none of the
Descendents here of those worthy Patriots who defended the
Liberty of their Country against all Invaders, who assisted the
great King Robert Bruce, to restore the Constitution and revenge
the Falshood of England and Usurpation of Baliol? Where are
the Douglasses and the Campbells? Where are the Peers; where

are the Barons, once the Bulwark of the Nation?') It will be remembered that it was Hamilton who had originally proposed that the nomination of the Commissioners for Union should be left to the Queen, which ensured that they recommended an incorporating Union. The puzzle of his behaviour—leading the opposition to the Union in Parliament yet at every crucial moment taking action that would prevent the Union from being blocked—has often been commented on.

Was it all a matter of jobbery and bribery, as has been so often maintained? Why did the Squadrone Volante, who had originally prided themselves on their independence, in the end vote solidly for the Union? That they were, in the modern phrase, 'leaned on' in one way or another seems pretty certain. But it is unlikely that there was outright bribery: political pressure, promise of office, indirect financial inducements there undoubtedly were. There was even in one respect at least a direct financial inducement, since in August 1706 a royal warrant was issued putting a loan of £20,000 at the disposal of the Government in Scotland, on the ground that debts and current expenses could not otherwise be met. The sum was paid in two instalments in October and November; over half went to defray the expenses of the Commissioner and his staff; the rest was said to have gone in paying arrears of salary that the Government had promised its friends and potential friends. Lockhart of Carnwath maintained that some people to whom no arrears were due received payment from this sum, but he is a prejudiced witness. There seems however to have been no direct naked payments to people for voting for the Government, and in at least one case—that of the Duke of Atholl, who is said to have received £1,000—money was apparently received by someone who voted against the Union.

Much more important than any possible bribery were concessions made by the Government to Scottish economic interests, at the instigation of Queensberry. In his letter to Godolphin of 7 November 1706, after noting that the Convention of Royal Boroughs had presented an address against Union, he added: 'After al wee hope, if the alterations be aloued, wee will carie it in

Parlament'. He goes on to say that although the Government has
a majority he hopes he can depend on, 'without thes alterations
nothing can be done that will pleas the treading peopel'. Although
for many Scots arguments of economic self-interest were out-
weighed by patriotic feeling, for many others (including the
lairds even more than the burgesses) the economic interests were
paramount. As T. C. Smout has summed it up: 'The international position of Scotland in the early eighteenth century was
too isolated, her internal weaknesses and divisions too acute and
wide-ranging, and the determination of England to protect herself
from these weaknesses by absorbing her neighbour too strong, to
offer much rational hope north of the Border that Scotland's
cherished independence could be long preserved.'

So although political and financial pressure was certainly
exerted, it was a long-term view of economic self-interest that
appears to have motivated most of those Scots who voted for the
Union. Several leading members of the Squadrone were genuinely
converted to this view. As early as November 1705 Roxburgh
wrote to Baillie of Jerviswood that he had been spending long
hours anxiously reflecting on arguments about the Union and
later he told him that he had changed his mind and no longer
believed that the Union was against Scotland's interest, having
been convinced by the way the English had been behaving in
'their late proceedings in relation to the Union'. Roxburgh's
change of mind was important in determining the attitude of the
Squadrone.

There was also the question of the jockeying for power by the
Scottish magnates, the Dukes of Hamilton, Queensberry, Atholl
and Argyll. The fact that each was after personal power and used
the cross-currents of politics in his own interests obscures the
actual political attitudes involved, as indeed it did to the English
Ministers who never fully understood the unstructured nature of
Scottish politics. They backed Queensberry and his men, whom
they considered good Whigs in their own sense of that term,
although, as T. I. Rae has argued, 'Queensberry was not a Whig
in anybody's terms—he was a magnate and did what seemed best

for himself'. And the Squadrone were not always motivated by
the kind of reasons that Roxburgh put to Jerviswood: when,
after the Union, in the 1707–8 session of the British Parliament,
they joined a section of the English Whigs to force the abolition
of the Scottish Privy Council in order to weaken the influence of
the English Court and the Court Party in Scotland, they were, as
again Rae has argued, 'deserting Godolphin to pay off old scores
against Queensberry and John, second Duke of Argyll'. Scottish
politics had for centuries been a more personal matter than the
(at least superficially) more logically structured party politics of
late seventeenth- and eighteenth-century England. After the
Union, when power was clearly in London and the small number
of Scottish members at Westminster diminished dramatically the
electoral influence of the magnates, the pattern of Scottish politics
temporarily turned to the English Whig versus Tory division,
but this did not last long, as there were special factors in the
Scottish situation—notably Jacobitism, and, of a very different
kind, the new centres of influence provided by the Court of
Session (now, like the Church, a symbol of Scottish nationhood
and a real centre of political power) and the post-Union legal
establishment generally.

The Jacobites, though their avowed aim was to bring James
Francis Edward (otherwise known as the Chevalier St George) to
the throne of all the Kingdoms that his father James VII and II had
lost, never accepted the Union. The death of Queen Anne on
1 August 1714 did not bring the Jacobite *coup* that many had
hoped for, and George I (son of Sophia Electress of Hanover) was
immediately established as King of Great Britain, with a Whig
government. When the Earl of Mar, who had strongly supported
the Union and had been Secretary of State for Scotland in the
last year of Queen Anne's reign, was dismissed from his secretaryship at King George's accession and then deliberately snubbed by
the King after he had presented him with a loyal address, he
turned Jacobite, having already turned against the Union. When
he raised James's standard at Braemar on 6 September 1715 in the
unsuccessful Jacobite rising of that year it is said that the blue

standard, with the Scottish arms wrought in gold on one side and the Scottish thistle on the other, bore above the thistle the ancient Scottish motto *Nemo me impune lacessit* ('No one injures me with impunity') and beneath it the words 'No Union'. When James' son Charles Edward attempted to gain the throne for his father in the rising of 1745-6, his various proclamations named him as 'Charles, Prince of Wales, &c. Regent of Scotland, England, France and Ireland, and the Dominions thereunto belonging' (the inclusion of France was because of the English King's traditional though totally unreal claim to the French throne; it was even more unreal when the Jacobites looked to the French King for help). But on only one occasion did these proclamations suggest an end to the Union: this was when Charles, having heard that Parliament had been summoned to meet at Westminster on 17 October 1745, issued a proclamation warning 'all his Majesty's Liege Subjects' not to obey the summons and adding specifically that 'those of his Majesty's Subjects of this his ancient Kingdom of Scotland' who presumed to sit or vote in that Parliament would be punished as traitors and rebels, 'the pretended Union of these Kingdoms being now at an end'.

In Scotland Jacobitism survived as a species of Scottish national-ism with inevitable anti-Union and often also anti-English implications (for Jacobitism persisted in Scotland, as a sentiment at least, in much greater force than it did in England). Article XXIV of the Treaty of Union provided that 'the Crown, Scepter and Sword of State' of Scotland should be kept in Scotland, but in fact they disappeared from view until 1818. When in January 1818 Walter Scott was planning to recover them from the 'mysterious chest' in Edinburgh Castle and have them publicly exhibited he wrote to the Duke of Buccleuch that he remembered the Jacobite and anti-Union sentiments of members of 'the rebel company which debauched my youth' and especially an anti-Union song which saw the Scottish crown after the Union used

> To make a can/ For brandie Nan
> To p— in when she's tipsy.

He quoted another stanza of the same song:

> Farewell thou ancient Kingdom
> Farewell thou ancient Kingdom
> Who sold thyself
> For English pelf
> Was ever such a thing done.

Jacobite songs were sometimes anti-Union, but not always. After 1745 they tended to centre on the person and fate of Bonnie Prince Charlie, and as the rising of that year receded in time Jacobitism became more and more a nostalgic sentiment rather than a serious political attitude. It was in the songs and poems circulated immediately after the Union was effected that we see Jacobitism and anti-unionism most often combined. One of the earliest anti-Union poems is the anonymous 'Verses on the Scots Peers 1706':

> Our Duiks were deills, our Marquesses wer mad,
> Our Earls were evills, our Viscounts yet more bad,
> Our Lords were villains, and our Barons knaves
> Who with our burrows did sell us for slaves.
>
> They sold the church, they sold the State and Nation,
> They sold their honour, name and reputation,
> They sold their birthright, peerages and places
> And now they leave the House with angrie faces . . .
>
> Let all true Scots with God importunant be
> That he may yet restore our pristine libertie;
> That he who rules the hearts of kings alone
> May settle James at length upon the throne.

The Jacobites were largely Episcopalians; on the whole, in spite of more than a century of divisions and disruptions that followed, the Church of Scotland accepted the Union, which guaranteed her status. But the anonymous 'Litanie anent the Union' shows how at first there were plenty of worried Presbyterians who feared that a Union with England meant domination by English prelacy:

> From a forced and divided Union
> And from the church and kirk communion
> Where Lordly prelates have dominion
>   Deliver us, Lord.
> From a new transubstantiation
> Of the old Scots into ane English nation
> And from all the foes to Reformation
>   Deliver us, Lord . . .
> From trading with ane emptie purse
> And meriting the old wife's curse,
> And from all changes to the worse
>   Deliver us, Lord.

Such fears proved groundless, and the complicated history of the Church of Scotland after the Union is largely the history of a national church facing its own problems. There were nevertheless Acts passed by the British Parliament soon after the Union that upset the Church. In March 1712 the Toleration Act was passed, giving freedom of worship to Scottish Episcopalians and permitting their use of the Book of Common Prayer. Orthodox Presbyterians regarded this as a 'licensing of schism, heresy and sedition'. Another clause in this Act prohibited the enforcement by a magistrate of any ecclesiastical summons or sentence, and this was objected to by William Carstares as giving the Church of Scotland 'no more power than a philosopher'. A further clause required every minister of the Church and every pastor of an Episcopal congregation to pray specifically for Queen Anne and for the Princess Sophia. It also required of all ministers and pastors an oath abjuring the Stewarts, which outraged the Jacobites to the same degree that toleration of Episcopalians in Scotland outraged the Presbyterians. The abjuration oath caused great controversy and bitterness in Scotland, for it also bound those who subscribed to it to accept the succession as defined in an Act that provided that the monarch must be a member of the

Church of England. Conflict between jurants and non-jurants almost produced a schism in the Church, which was prevented only by a re-phrasing of the Act in 1719, omitting reference to the Act of Settlement.

Soon after the Toleration Act came an Act that produced even more controversy in Scotland, though it was less bitterly opposed at the time. This was the Patronage Act of 1712, restoring the right of lay patrons to appoint ministers. The issue of lay patronage had been a divisive one ever since the establishment of Protestantism in Scotland, where it had been recognized as early as 1567, offensive though it was to many of the Presbyterian clergy. But its restoration in 1712—widely regarded, as was the Toleration Act, as a branch of the Treaty of Union—produced a running sore in the Church of Scotland. It brought an element of class division into the question of church government and was a fruitful source of schism and controversy, culminating in the Disruption of 1843, when three hundred ministers of the Church of Scotland walked out of the General Assembly, in protest against its decision to uphold the Government on the patronage question, to form the Free Church of Scotland under Thomas Chalmers.

Another Act of the Westminster Parliament that was regarded as directed against the Church of Scotland, though in a much more petty manner, was the Yule Vacance Act, deliberately exacerbating the feelings of Presbyterians, who regarded Christmas as Popish, by restoring the Christmas recess in the law courts. It was repealed after a few years. A more serious breach of the Treaty of Union—or so it was widely regarded in Scotland—was the refusal of a seat in the House of Lords to the Duke of Hamilton after he had been created Duke of Brandon in the peerage of Great Britain in 1711, which did indeed seem to be in flat contradiction of Article XXIII of the Treaty. The matter was not resolved until 1782, when the then Duke of Hamilton and Brandon was granted a seat in the Lords: after that all Scottish peers who were peers of Great Britain were able to sit in the Lords.

Some breaches of the Treaty of Union were clearly on the side of humanity and progress and represent development that would have taken place anyway. The Heritable Jurisdictions Act of 1747, abolishing the judicial offices held as private property, reformed the Sheriff courts and improved the administration of justice in Scotland, even though it was passed as the direct result of the Jacobite rising of 1745. And all legislation after the Union that weakened the monopoly of the Church of Scotland was in breach of the Act for Securing the Protestant Religion and Presbyterian Church Government that was incorporated in the Treaty of Union. Thus various educational reforms, notably the Scottish Universities Act of 1858, which radically reorganized the structure of the Scottish universities, implicitly removed the religious test in the appointment of teachers and administrators that had been promised in the Act 'for ever'. Such moves towards toleration were part of a general move towards a more pluralistic culture and cannot be regarded directly as a consequence of the Union. At the same time the reform of Scottish university traditional teaching practice and curricula to bring them closer into line with the practice of Oxford and Cambridge would probably not have come about in a Scotland that had retained its independence.

On the question of appeals to the House of Lords from the Court of Session and the High Court of Justiciary the Treaty of Union was silent. All that was said (in Article XIX) was 'that no Causes in Scotland be cognoscible by the Courts of Chancery, Queens-Bench, Common-Pleas, or any other Court in Westminsterhall; And that the said Courts, or any other of the like nature after the Union, shall have no power to Cognosce, Review or Alter the Acts or Sentences of the Judicatures within Scotland, or stop the Execution of the same'. The practice of appealing from the Court of Session to the House of Lords nevertheless did develop, most notoriously in the case of James Greenshields, an Episcopal clergyman who in 1711 successfully appealed to the Lords against his condemnation by the Court of Session for using an Anglican prayer-book in Edinburgh. (It was this successful appeal that lay behind the Toleration Act of 1712.)

Many Scotsmen regarded the outcome of the Greenshields case as a flagrant breach of the guarantee in the Treaty of Union of the Church of Scotland's exclusive position. But the practice of appealing to the Lords continued, and in 1730 was mentioned by Sir John Clerk of Penicuik as one of the complaints voiced in Scotland since the Union. Since no judge with training in Scots Law sat in the House of Lords before the middle of the nineteenth century, Scottish appeals were heard by the Lord Chancellor and English lawyer peers who were generally quite ignorant of Scots Law. It is true that Scotsmen appealing to the Lords could be represented there by a Scots advocate (James Boswell represented a Scots client in the Lords in 1772), but as late as 1858 a Lord Chancellor of Britain (Lord Cranworth) could exclaim, in deciding in the case of Bartonshill Coal Company v. Reid that the English doctrine of common employment should also apply to Scotland, 'if such be the law of England on what ground can it be argued not to be the law of Scotland?'

The ecclesiastical schisms that developed in Scotland after the Union and culminated in the Disruption of 1843 involved social and cultural as well as doctrinal factors that were already developing before the Union and would have manifested themselves anyway. Many regarded the rigorous Presbyterian elements in Scotland, including those who joined the Free Church of Scotland, as peculiarly representative of Scottish national character. Generations of writers in the eighteenth and nineteenth centuries took this view. But those on the other side, the Moderates, among whom were the *literati* of eighteenth-century Edinburgh, the leaders of the Scottish Enlightenment, also typified their nation, if in a very different way. And there was the continuing Episcopalian-Jacobite tradition, which had a good claim to be the true tradition of Scotland (Walter Scott joined the Scottish Episcopal Church because it represented continuity with the Scottish past); it was especially strong in Aberdeenshire. This tradition satisfied some national instincts that the sterner Presbyterian tradition stifled. In the north generally Episcopalians and Catholics kept up Gaelic while Presbyterian ministers often tried to stamp it out. Scottish Episcopalians were more in touch with Scotland's mediaeval past than any Protestants in the Covenanting tradition could possibly be. They bore no blame for the destruction of abbeys and churches and the suppressing of popular literature and festivities.

As for the Gaelic-speaking Highlands, they had really little to do with the Union one way or another. The association of many (though far from all) of the clans with Jacobitism and the decisive defeat of the Jacobites at Culloden in 1746, which ended the Jacobite movement as a political force once and for all, was seen in England, and indeed by many in Lowland Scotland, as the defeat of an uncouth and primitive race by representatives of civilization and progress. To this day it is common to see references to Culloden as a great defeat of a Scottish by an English army. The truth is much more complicated. There were Scots on both sides. The division between the social structure and culture of Lowland Scotland and the social structure and culture of the Gaelic-speaking Highlands had been increasing for generations before the rising of 1745, in spite of General Wade's road-building in the Highlands between 1726 and 1733, and his enlisting of loyal clans into Highland Companies. After Culloden, every effort was made by the British Government to destroy the old patterns of society and culture in the Gaelic-speaking Highlands and in Professor Smout's phrase 'convert the Highland population to Lowland values'. Though the power to do this was largely (if not exclusively) supplied by the English, it was an assimilation of the Highlands to Lowland Scottish ways that was the objective. Of course, Anglicizing forces had been working in Lowland Scotland for centuries, so it was not always easy to distinguish between the English and the Lowland Scottish elements. But it should be said that the Highland Clearances and other methods of destroying Highland society that were carried out at the end of the eighteenth and in the first half of the nineteenth centuries were carried out by Scottish chiefs and lairds, with the support of the legal and ecclesiastical establishment in Scotland, in the name of 'improvement'.

Walter Scott, writing in 1814 in the final chapter of *Waverley*, looked back with a mixture of nostalgia and complacency:

There is no European nation which, within the course of half a century, or little more, has undergone so complete a change as this kingdom of Scotland. The effects of the insurrection of 1745—the destruction of the patriarchal power of the Highland chiefs—the abolition of the heritable jurisdictions of the Lowland nobility and barons [in 1747]—the total eradication of the Jacobite party, which, averse to intermingle with the English, or adopt their customs, long continued to pride themselves upon maintaining ancient Scottish manners and customs—commenced this innovation. The gradual influx of wealth and extension of commerce, have since united to render the present people of Scotland a class of beings as different from their grandfathers as the existing English are from those of Queen Elizabeth's time.

A modern historian, Eric Cregeen, has made a similar point with a different emphasis: 'What destroyed the old highland social and political structure was its growing involvement in the general cultural influence of neighbours to the south, England and Scottish lowlands. This influence, expressed in speech, manners, clothes, religion, political sympathy and activity, trade, seasonal migration, and so on, was at work in the highlands a long time before 1745, and reached its climax considerably after.'

When General Wade arrived in Scotland in 1725 with a Government commission to investigate the whole state of the Highlands, the Shawfield riots were going on in Glasgow, in protest against the Government's new malt tax. These riots, which like the Porteous riot in Edinburgh in 1736 were at bottom directed against the Union although sparked off by a more immediate issue, seriously disturbed the Government, which ordered the Lord Advocate, Duncan Forbes of Culloden, to send frequent reports on the situation to the Duke of Newcastle and asked the Earl of Islay (who succeeded his brother as Duke of Argyll in 1743: the family were still powerful in Scotland) to bring pressure on the Scottish judges to take all necessary action. Islay was acting for the British Prime Minister, Walpole, and

Walpole used the situation in Scotland as a means of forcing out of his Cabinet the Duke of Roxburgh, the Squadrone member and Secretary of State for Scotland.

Was Scotland, then, after the Union regarded by the Westminster Government simply as a troublesome northern region that had to be kept from upsetting the established order and whose affairs could be used as instruments in jockeying for power among Ministers in London? To some extent this is true, as it was true of William's view of Scotland and even to some extent of the view of James VI and I after 1603. When in 1709, after a bitter debate in Parliament, an Act was passed assimilating the law of treason in Scotland to that which had prevailed in England since the time of Edward I (and which had been used by Edward against Wallace), it became clear that Westminster could not tolerate the idea of Scots law being different in this crucial respect, whatever the Act of Union said. (It was under this Act that the Jacobite rebels of 1745–6 were executed.) But on the whole there was little direct attempt by Westminster to legislate away the peculiarities of the Scottish system. The 1727 Act establishing the Commissioners and Trustees for Improveing Fisherys and Manufactures in Scotland was prepared by the Convention of Royal Burghs and 'improving' Scottish landlords. The Election Act of 1743, aimed at suppressing corruption in Scottish elections, was drafted by the Scottish law officers before being forwarded to Parliament, as was the Entail Act of 1770 (aimed at abolishing the mandatory short leases that had been the bane of Scottish agriculture for centuries). Even the Heritable Jurisdictions Act of 1747, which the Scottish judges refused to draft at the request of Lord Chancellor Hardwicke, was not in its objectives a subject of disagreement between Scottish and the English law officers: the judges' refusal stemmed from their objection to becoming involved in arguments about the amount of compensation to be given to the landowners whose heritable jurisdictions were to be abolished.

The abolition of the Scottish Privy Council in 1708 severed an important link between London and Edinburgh. Sir John Clerk of

Penicuik, writing on the state of Scotland in 1730, noted the complaint (chiefly voiced by the nobility, who had dominated it, though Clerk does not say this)

> that by takeing away the Privy Council of Scotland there is very little of Government to be seen amongst us. This complaint I am affray'd is too well founded, for tho' the peace of the country be in the hands of certain justices of peace as in England, yet there are some shires in this country where they doe not meet at all, and there are others where I am affray'd they meet to oppress one another either as justices of the peace or as commissioners of supply ... Tho' the Privy Council was frequently arbitrary, and tho' there was noe necessity for a sett of men to be constituted under that name after the councils of Britain fell to be united in 1707, yet considering our distance from the seat of Government I cannot help thinking that it wou'd be of very great use for preserving the peace and ease of this country and the better collecting and inbringing of His Majesties Revenue that some expedient was thought on for supplying this defect.

Walpole's political manœuvring in response to the Glasgow rioting over the malt tax and the serious unrest it indicated resulted in the dropping of Roxburgh as Secretary of State for Scotland and the lapsing of that office until 1746. The Duke of Argyll and his brother the Earl of Islay for a while virtually ran Scotland between them. On the fall of Walpole in 1742 the Secretaryship of State for Scotland was revived and given to the fourth Marquis of Tweeddale, a political opponent of Islay. Islay succeeded his brother as Duke of Argyll in 1743 and out-manœuvred the ineffective Tweeddale to become (in Horace Walpole's words) 'the supreme authority in Scotland'. Tweeddale was ousted from the Secretaryship in 1746 and the office again lapsed until the creation of a Scottish Office headed by a Secretary for Scotland in 1885.

So the managing of Scotland in the interests of the Government at Westminster was in the years immediately after the Union in the hands either of a Secretary for Scotland or of a magnate powerful enough or clever enough to convince the Government that he was running Scotland in their interests. Eventually, however, it became clear that it was the legal establishment in Scotland who were the natural holders of power and dispensers of patronage in that country. First there was the abolition of the Privy Council, then (partly as a result of this) the lapsing of the Secretaryship for Scotland, then the bidding for power by individual magnates, and finally the emergence of the Lord Advocate, the chief Scottish law officer and, as such, the link between the Scottish legal administration and the Government, as the main dispenser of patronage in Scotland. The career of Henry Dundas, first Viscount Melville (1742–1811) illustrates with particular vividness the way in which Scotland could be governed by a strong-minded member of the Scottish legal establishment who had the confidence of the ministry in London. Dundas was Lord Advocate from 1775 to 83, and from 1783 to 1805, during which period he held a variety of high offices, the uncrowned king of Scotland, 'King Harry the Ninth'. Other members of his family held important posts, his elder brother Robert (1713–87) becoming Lord President of the Court of Session in 1760 and his nephew, Robert Dundas of Arniston (1758–1819) becoming Lord Advocate in 1789. The Dundas power in Scotland was made possible not only by the character and ambitions of the Dundases themselves but also by the role the Scottish legal establishment had come to play in representing the Government in Scotland. This role was made possible by the provision in the Treaty of Union maintaining the Scottish legal system unchanged after the Union. But the peculiar prestige and importance of the law in Scotland after the Union were part of the whole social and cultural pattern that developed in the eighteenth century, and that requires separate discussion.

11. Consequences

The economic benefits of the Union, so eloquently prophesied by its supporters, were slow to manifest themselves. Significant economic advancement in Scotland after the Union dates from about 1730. True, the Equivalent, fixed in Article XXV of the Treaty of Union as £398,085 10s., was duly paid, though only after some confusion and delay, and it was mainly spent on paying the public debts of the Scottish Crown and in compensating the stockholders of the Company of Scotland trading to Africa and the Indies for their losses: what was left eventually formed part of the initial capital of the Board of Commissioners and Trustees for Improveing Fisherys and Manufactures in Scotland set up in 1727. Sir John Clerk of Penicuik in 1730 listed Scotland's chief exports before the Union as wool (whose export he deplored as enriching the merchants but impoverishing ordinary people, as little or nothing was left to be manufactured in Scotland); linen; black cattle (exported to England); fish (but he considered the markets lost through bad management); worsted stockings from Aberdeenshire; and some miscellaneous items of less importance. After the Union he noted an increase in the export of black cattle to England, an improvement in linen manufactures ('in propor-tion to the care that was taken of them') and some increase in the export of herring. Woollen manufactures were 'in much the same condition as at the time of the Union'.

One more immediate economic effect of the Union was to call a halt to the progressive worsening of the financial situation. 'Before the Union,' wrote Clerk, 'in the years 1703, 1704, 1705 this country was in greater distress for want of money than it has been even for these many years.' This 'dearth of monies' was to be a continuing problem, but at least the reform of the Scottish Exchequer that followed on the Union helped to make possible an improvement in the situation. The transfer of taxation after the Union caused loud complaint, and we have already noted the fierce response to the malt tax of 1725. But this tax only produced £20,000 for transmission to London: after 1727 any amount over that was transferred to the Board of Trustees for Improveing Fisherys and Manufactures for purposes of economic development in Scotland. It has been calculated that in the half century after the Union no more than from 15 to 20 per cent of the revenue raised in Scotland went south to serve United Kingdom purposes.

The most tangible economic effect of the Union was its opening of the tobacco trade with the American colonies to Glasgow merchants. Here they soon outstripped their English rivals in Whitehaven, Lancaster, Liverpool and Bristol, the amount of imported tobacco rising from about $2\frac{1}{2}$ million lbs in 1715 to 4 million in 1728, to over 47 million in 1771, by which time the Clyde was importing more than half of all the tobacco that came to Britain. (Most of it was re-exported.) It was the Virginia tobacco trade that produced the wealthy Glasgow 'tobacco lords' of the eighteenth century. Even before the spectacular rise of tobacco imports Glasgow merchants developed trade with the West Indies, importing sugar and its by-products, molasses and rum. The first of Glasgow's main sources of prosperity in the eighteenth century to develop was the sugar trade; then came tobacco; then the development of the fine linen industry and, towards the end of the century, of the cotton industry brought a surge of new population into Glasgow not only from the surrounding districts but also from the West Highlands.

The development of the textile industry in Scotland was deliberately encouraged by the Government after the Union. The Board of Trustees for Improveing Fisherys and Manufactures in Scotland devoted itself energetically to the development of the Scottish linen industry and its encouragement of improved standards of weaving and of new techniques of manufacture were important factors in the remarkable growth of the industry throughout the country. The Convention of Royal Burghs (guaranteed survival in Article XXI of the Treaty of Union) also interested itself in promoting trade and manufactures, and made special efforts to help both the linen industry and herring fishing. The Forfeited Estates Commissioners, appointed in 1752 to manage the estates forfeited by Jacobite rebels after the rebellion of 1745, also exerted themselves to assist Scottish manufactures, especially in the Highlands: in 1753 Parliament granted from the proceeds of these estates an annual sum of £3,000 for nine years to help the linen industry in the Highlands. And in 1754 there was founded the Edinburgh Society for Encouraging Arts, Sciences, Manufactures, and Agriculture, which not only discussed Scotland's economic problems but also offered prizes for conspicuous agricultural and industrial achievement.

It was the primitive state of agriculture that presented Scotland's greatest economic problem at the time of the Union. Land throughout the country was still cultivated on the primitive and wasteful infield and outfield system, and tenants owned scattered strips or 'rigs' of land, generally crooked S-shaped ridges flanked by banks of weeds. The old wooden plough, which required a team of eight or twelve oxen to draw it, was still in wide use. Harrows were also wooden and pulled by hand; corn was threshed with the flail and ground in mills to which tenants were bound to take their corn and pay lavishly for having it ground and even for not having it ground. Shortage of winter cattle-feed led to a high mortality of cattle and sheep during the winter.

Agricultural improvement went on sporadically and unevenly, but very definitely, throughout the century, under the influence of the example of Holland, where so many budding lawyers went from Scotland to study Roman Law, on which much Scots law was based, and of England, where visiting Scottish landowners picked up not only new agricultural methods but also English farmers to advise and help. To improve methods of farming on one's estate, to import seeds, to plant trees, even to lay out a new planned village—these became favourite preoccupations of the more enlightened Scottish gentry in the eighteenth century and sometimes went along with an interest in literature and the arts. These men, often paternalistic and enlightened 'improvers', were often also industrial entrepreneurs. 103 Glasgow tobacco merchants owned between them 145 estates between 1770 and 1815, and many of them set out to farm them in the most efficient and rational way. It was this infusion of new blood into agriculture that brought the traditional power of the landowner on to the side of economic reform and helped to transform Scottish agriculture from a passively accepted inherited way of life into a variety of capitalist enterprise. How much the Union was directly related to this development is arguable. But that it was related to the whole movement of the Scottish Enlightenment, and that the Scottish Enlightenment had something to do with the after-effects of the Union, is indisputable.

One can distinguish two different yet related reactions to the Union on the cultural side. The first was what might be called a patriotic nostalgia, and the second was a determination that now that Scotland was North Britain its writers and thinkers should show the world that it could represent Britain proudly in the eyes of Europe and indeed beat the English at their own game by producing works of international importance written in a pure and elegant English style. The first of these two reactions produced antiquarianism; collecting, editing and imitating of older Scottish poetry; and a variety of activities designed to turn attention to the days when Scotland was an independent kingdom with a lively literary culture of its own. The second produced that galaxy of historians, philosophers, literary critics, scientists and scholars that we call the Scottish Enlightenment. The first looked back to the time when Scots was a full-blooded literary language of its own and not regarded simply as a group of northern dialects of English, and resulted not only in collections and editions of older Scottish poetry but also in imitations of such poetry, particularly on the popular level (ballads and folk songs) and the writing of an original Scots poetry that was partly based on existing Scottish dialects, partly on the usage of older Scottish poets (particularly those that had come down in oral tradition or in vulgarized form in chap-books) and partly on the standard English that was now regarded as the proper form of public written speech. The second looked entirely to standard English as its method of expression and was happier in expository prose than in poetry. Burns represented some aspects of the first; David Hume was perhaps the most distinguished representative of the second. Scott, with his antiquarian passion, his interest in history and in the ways in which the past modulated into the present, and his simultaneous belief in progress and improvement, combined both reactions and out of the resulting tensions within his own mind and imagination was able to invent the historical novel.

A clear sign of the emergence of the first of these two movements appeared in 1706, the year in which the debate about the Union reached its climax and in which it became plain that the Treaty of Union would be passed. This was the first of James Watson's three volumes entitled *A Choice Collection of Comic and Serious Scots Poems both Ancient and Modern*, of which the second and third volumes appeared in 1709 and 1711. Watson was an ardent Scottish patriot who had got into trouble in 1700 for printing a pamphlet entitled *People of Scotland's Groans and Lamentable Complaints Pour'd out before the High Court of Parliament*. His prefatory note to the first volume of the *Choice Collection* made clear his motives: he describes the work as 'the first of its Nature which has been publish'd in our own native Scots dialect'. Watson's collection in fact (except for ballads, which it lacked, and song lyrics, of which it included few, and the perhaps surprising omission of anything by Sir David Lindsay) represented fairly accurately the different kinds of material available for the development or reconstruction of a Scottish poetic tradition in the eighteenth century. Later collectors and editors throughout the ensuing century, from Allan Ramsay's *Tea-Table Miscellany* and *The Evergreen* (both 1724) to Walter Scott's *Minstrelsy of the Scottish Border* (1802–3), made good Watson's omissions in a variety of ways, although the emphasis in the great majority of these collections was on the Scottish folk tradition rather than on the sophisticated 'art' tradition of the late mediaeval Scottish makars. The reason for this was largely that ever since the departure of the Court and of Court patronage of the arts from Edinburgh in 1603, Court poetry and Court music had declined, some of it turning up later in simplified form in popular broadsheets and chap-books, but the bulk of it simply replaced by works in the popular tradition. But even these works, long bitterly opposed by the sterner elements of the Presbyterian church in Scotland, had often been pushed underground, to be fragmented, or distorted, or maimed or simply lost; which was why so many eighteenth-century Scottish collectors and editors (notably David Herd, whose two-volume edition of *Ancient and Modern Scottish Songs* published in 1776, was a valiant attempt to record faithfully all that survived of Scottish popular sung poetry, and nourished the imagination of both Burns and Scott) tried so hard to assemble, improve and in the case of Burns even re-create this poetry.

Ramsay's *Tea-Table Miscellany* was a collection of Scottish songs and ballads, some re-written in neo-classic English, others 'improved' in a variety of ways, others again printed from broadsides or other sources as Ramsay found them. It reflects a certain cultural confusion in Ramsay's own mind. In *The Evergreen* Ramsay introduced his readers to the great poetry of late mediaeval Scotland, that of Dunbar and Henryson in particular, taking most of his material from the sixteenth-century Bannatyne Manuscript. There was a patriotic motive here. In his preface Ramsay wrote: 'When these good old Bards wrote, we had not made Use of imported Trimmings upon our Cloaths, nor of foreign Embroidery in our Writings. Their Poetry is the product of their own Country, not pilfered and spoiled in the Transportation from abroad: Their Images are native, and their Landskips domestick; copied from those Fields and Meadows we every Day behold.' He introduced fiercely patriotic poems of his own, written in an archaic style and attributed to the sixteenth-century Scottish poet Alexander Scott: one of these laments the oppression of Scotland by England and prophesies a successful fight for the re-establishment of an independent kingdom of

Scotland. Significantly, it is set in 1300, at the height of the Scottish War of Independence against England. The fact that when attacking the Union and preaching Scottish independence Ramsay did not have the courage to speak in his own person is significant. Eighteenth-century Scottish nationalism became more and more associated with antiquarianism as the ineluctable fact of the Union became more and more evident and it was clear that any political fight against it belonged to the past. It was partly this realization that produced the move from politics to literature that we find both in the antiquarian movement and in the Scottish Enlightenment.

Associated with what we might call the patriotic antiquarian movement was a kind of scholarly patriotic publishing represented especially by Robert Freebairn and Thomas Ruddiman. Freebairn, son of a Bishop of Edinburgh who had to turn to bookselling after the Revolution of 1689, both edited and printed Henry Maule's *The History of the Picts* (1706), Gavin Douglas's translation of Virgil's *Aeneid* (1710) and the *Opera Omnia* (complete works) of the sixteenth-century Scottish humanist George Buchanan. These and other of his publications, including Thomas Crawford's *Notes and Observations on Mr. George Buchanan's History of Scotland* and Patrick Abercromby's *Martial Achievements of the Scottish Nation*, reflected the passionate desire on the part of a number of Scots, in the years of the Union debate and immediately afterwards, to re-interpret Scottish history in such a way as both to satisfy outraged national pride and explain exactly what had happened. Scottish men of letters were drawn to history in the eighteenth century in a way that no other writers in Europe were, because they were obsessed with what had happened to their country (as Scott was, but in his case the obsession led him to historical fiction). But it is the emphasis on indigenous Scottish classical scholarship co-existing with nationalist feeling that distinguishes the publications of Freebairn and Ruddiman.

Ruddiman came from the Episcopalian and Jacobite north-east of Scotland, where there was also a strong classical tradition, nurtured at Aberdeen, which had long been producing its own

Latin grammarians and its own ways of studying grammar and rhetoric. The influence on him of the physician and poet Dr Archibald Pitcairne (1652–1715), himself a proficient writer of Latin verse, brought him from Aberdeen to Edinburgh, where he worked for Freebairn (he did much of the work for Freebairn's edition of Douglas's *Aeneid*) before setting up as a printer on his own. He produced his influential *Rudiments of the Latin Tongue* in 1714 and worked on Freebairn's edition of Buchanan's *Opera Omnia* in 1715. In 1728 he became joint-printer to the University of Edinburgh and in 1730 he was appointed Keeper of the Advocates Library; he compiled its catalogue and published the first volume in 1742. He edited and published much other work of Scottish historical and classical interest, Tory, Jacobite and Episcopalian in tone where editorial apparatus allowed him to show his own views, and engaged in polemics with Whig interpreters of Scottish history. He championed a movement in Scottish culture that can be called *vernacular humanism* (using 'humanism' in the old Renaissance sense), which saw Latin rather than English as Scotland's international cultural language and represented a tradition in Scottish culture that had existed at least since Buchanan. He tried to mould it into a shape in which it could do something to compensate for the Union and the consequent loss of Scottish national identity.

Vernacular humanism was short-lived in eighteenth-century Scotland, yet it left its effects. While a poet like Allan Ramsay and even Burns turned to Scots as a sort of compensation for an avowed ignorance of Latin and Greek, one eighteenth-century Scottish poet, Robert Fergusson (who comes between Ramsay and Burns), who was educated at Dundee Grammar School and St Andrews University, was at home in the classics and in the Ruddiman tradition. When he wrote in Scots he was able, when he wanted, to infuse into it a kind of *gravitas* that came from his being at home in Latin. Even in his poems describing the life and colour and squalor of the Edinburgh of his day he could infuse a verbal richness that reminds us, though at a considerably lower level, of what the mediaeval makars were able to do with Scots.

This was something beyond the reach of Ramsay and the many contemporary patronizing or nostalgic or pastiche-writing dabblers in Scots verse, as it was beyond the reach of Burns, finer poet (at his best) than Fergusson though he was.

Scottish cultural pride could not, however, be restored after the Union by a vernacular humanism, a Scoto-Latin approach to Europe: it was altogether too late in the day for that. For all eighteenth-century Europe's esteem for classical culture, the objective was—in England as in France—to transmute it into a neo-classic style in the national language, and the leaders of the Scottish Enlightenment accepted this aim too, and accepted standard English as their national language. Sir David Dalrymple, Lord Hailes, Scottish judge, historian, critic and editor, who published his *Annals of Scotland* in 1776, contributed to Henry Mackenzie's polite magazine *The Mirror*, collected Scottish ballads, and edited *Ancient Scottish Poems from the Manuscript of George Bannatyne* in 1770, not only bridged the vernacular humanist movement and the nostalgic antiquarian movement but also brought elements of both of these into the Scottish Enlightenment, of which he was a distinguished representative.

'Is it not strange', wrote David Hume to Gilbert Elliot of Minto in July 1757, 'that, at a time when we have lost our Princes, our Parliaments, our independent Government, even the Presence of our chief Nobility, are unhappy, in our Accent & Pronunciation, speak a very corrupt Dialect of the Tongue, which we make use of; is it not strange, I say, that in these Circumstances, we shou'd really be the People most distinguish'd for Literature in Europe?' This mixture of pride in Scottish intellectual achievement with an ashamed view of the Scots language as 'a very corrupt dialect' is typical of one aspect of the Scottish Enlightenment. Scots had indeed now degenerated from the rich literary language with a living relationship to the spoken language that it had once been to a group of regional spoken dialects employed for the most part in antiquarian or local or deliberately low-life or nostalgic or merely imitative verses, but the view that it was a 'corrupt' form of English was strangely unhistorical to be held by a man who was both historian and philosopher. But such a view was bound up with the ambitions of the Scottish *literati* to perform before Europe in flawless English. Hume himself—whose spoken accent was said by someone who had heard them both speak to be more distinctively Scots than that of Burns—sent his manuscripts to English friends to be corrected of any Scotticisms, while Professor James Beattie of Aberdeen produced in 1787 (the very year when Burns was being lionized in Edinburgh after the publication in 1786 of his volume of *Poems, Chiefly in the Scottish Dialect*) his significantly titled book, *Scotticisms, arranged in Alphabetical Order, designed to correct Improprieties of Speech and Writing*, to help Scotsmen to rid themselves of anything Scots in their language. The interesting point is that most of the *literati*, however anxious they were to rid themselves of Scotticisms in their writing, preserved in their spoken language a distinctively Scottish form of speech. Their written English tended to be precise, formal and often rather rhetorical. This situation with respect to language—where, as Edwin Muir once put it, a Scotsman felt in Scots and thought in English—had been developing even before the Union, but there can be no doubt that the Union intensified it.

Scottish formal education was now entirely in English. Young Robert Burns, son of an Ayrshire tenant farmer, was taught by his young teacher John Murdoch to read and appreciate the English writers from Shakespeare to Gray and Shenstone, and to write a formal, correct, elegant English. It was Burns's combination of kinds of poetic craftsmanship that he found in the English poets with the Scottish folk tradition and elements of the Scottish formal literary tradition that formed the basis of the special kind of Scots poetry that he wrote. It was a remarkable achievement, but a balancing act that proved impossible for future generations, who turned Burns into a sentimental celebrator of Scottish rural life and in orgies of patriotic nostalgia, indulged in facile imitations of his more sentimental side. This went on right through the nineteenth and early twentieth century, and was responsible for the repudiation of Burns's influence and the cry 'Back to Dunbar' voiced by Hugh MacDiarmid, the leader of the Scottish poetic renaissance in the present century. This renaissance was many-sided, but in one of its aspects it attempted to solve Scotland's linguistic problem (which was now simply that most people spoke a rather Scottish English while they wrote an English English, while rural areas retained in addition to their Scottish pronunciation a considerable Scots vocabulary that they were not allowed to use at school) by welding elements from the older Scots language together with modern rural Scots and standard English into a new poetic language.

The eighteenth-century *literati* who were ashamed of their Scottish speech were nevertheless patriotic Scotsmen. David Hume (who found himself more at home in Paris than in London) was a great champion of his native land and was immensely proud of Scotland's cultural achievements in his own time. These achievements were indeed remarkable. The aim of the *literati*—to assert their country's claim to greatness by operating in the van of European progress in order to show that Scotland, small and poor though she might be and chequered though her history might have been, could proudly represent Britain before the world—was realized not only in philosophy, history and literary criticism, in the works of Hume himself, William Robertson, Hugh Blair, Lord Kames and others. It was also realized in sociology—virtually founded by eighteenth-century Scots—political economy, architecture, portrait painting, medi-cine, geology, chemistry and even road-building. (One need only mention Dugald Stewart, Adam Smith, Robert Adam, Sir Henry Raeburn, the dynasty of the doctors Monro, James Hutton, Joseph Black and John Loudon McAdam.) The Scottish Enlighten-ment was both philosophical and technological. It stood for belief in reason and progress, and for 'moderatism' in religion—really a somewhat optimistic deism presented as Christianity. It was an essentially genteel tradition, Scottish gentility, which was born in the eighteenth century and still survives, being a curiously defensive posture stemming from a simultaneous attempt to

repudiate the vulgarities of vernacular Scots, demonstrate the
advantages of education and social propriety, and assert a Scottish
presence. At a lower social level, in oyster cellars and taverns,
more riotous forms of urban Scottish life went on. While the
literati got genteelly muddled on claret, less pretentious members
of society consumed tipenny ale or whisky over rizzard haddocks.
The development of the social structure in Scottish cities, particularly in Edinburgh, after the Union presents a fascinating
spectacle.

Part of that spectacle is visible in Edinburgh's New Town, so
elegantly designed and neo-classically constructed in the late
eighteenth and early nineteenth centuries. Immediately before its
development, there had been Edinburgh's first New Town
(though never known as such), represented by Brown Square and
George Square and the whole area to the south and south-east of
the Cowgate. The buildings here were in what might be called a
vernacular neo-classic style, comparable to the vernacular humanism represented by Ruddiman, and distinct from the more international neo-classic style of the New Town to the north. It was
one of the most distinctive and effective aspects of post-Union
Edinburgh: most of it has recently been deliberately destroyed,
stone by stone, to make way for high-rise university buildings
and other unsuitable erections.

The gold medal awarded for the best plan for Edinburgh's New
Town went to James Craig in 1767. Craig's plan represented a
vision of an ideal city laid out with a rationality, an elegance and a
symmetry that mirrored the intellectual ideas of the Scottish
Enlightenment. Craig was a nephew of the poet James Thomson,
who had left his native Scotland to seek his literary fortune in
England, and he appended to his plan the following lines from
the concluding part of his uncle's poem, 'Liberty':

> August, around, what Public Works I see!
> Lo! stately Streets, lo! Squares that court the breeze!
> See long Canals and deepened Rivers join
> Each part with each, and with the circling Main
> The whole enlivened Isle.

These lines are spoken in Thomson's poem by the Goddess of Liberty who prophesies a glorious future for British arts and manufactures. It is a vision of 'the whole enlivened isle', of a prosperous united Britain. Edinburgh's splendid New Town, now such a striking and rightly admired part of the city that it seems to be part of its very spirit, was originally conceived as a British scene, a post-Union North British contribution to the glory of Britannia. It was Thomson, after all, who wrote 'Rule, Britannia!' and it was the Scots who talked (and still talk) of the whole island as 'Britain', while the English (and foreigners) obstinately talk of Britain as 'England'. Scotland surrendered its independence as a nation to become part of a flourishing Britain, and expected that if Scotland became North Britain then England should become South Britain. It did not work out that way.

Of course the picture is far more complicated than this. There was also a Scottish national pride in the designing and building of Edinburgh New Town and in the designation of the city as the 'Athens of the North'. Feelings in fact were ambivalent. One long-term result of the Union was the development of this kind of ambivalence of feeling among Scotsmen, a mixture of pride and shame (we see it precisely in James Boswell), a mingled desire to be British and to be known as Scots. But most of all the Union was responsible for making nostalgia the most characteristic Scottish emotion. This persisted right through the nineteenth century and is still present in our own time, as anyone who looks at a television programme of popular Scottish singing and dancing will at once see. Nostalgia is not a healthy emotion for a country. It can encourage the most outrageous sentimentalism and the most facile responses. Add to this the factor of exile, with Scots either being forced to emigrate for economic reasons (as in the Highland Clearances) or taking advantage of the existence of the British Empire to go out and make good in distant parts of the world, and you have a powerful mixture.

There was still another factor. This was an element of self-mockery, to be seen in the innumerable Scottish jokes (for example, about mean Aberdonians watching their bawbees) manufactured in and exported from Scotland, in the late-nineteenth and early-twentieth-century 'Scotch comic', with his extraordinary mixture of Lowland accent and Highland garb. Side by side with this music-hall view of the Scots there developed the romanticizing of the Highlands, which was mixed up with their development as a tourist attraction and a centre for deer-stalking and grouse-shooting by wealthy (often absentee) land-owners and their southern guests. It was Scott, in his narrative poem *The Lady of the Lake*, who opened up the Trossachs as a tourist area, and the process of touristizing (if one may coin a word) the Highlands got a new stimulus when Queen Victoria built her Scottish baronial castle at Balmoral in the 1850s. The whole process of what might be called Balmoralization, with the associated burgeoning of the tourist trade in tartanry and the mixing up of all this with the kilt, whisky (after the development and popularization of blended Scotch whisky in the latter part of the nineteenth century), haggis and the Road to the Isles, represented an extraordinary distortion of the history of Scottish culture and an ignorant confusion of wholly separate elements in that history.

As all this was developing, Glasgow was growing into a massive industrial city and Clydeside became famous for shipbuilding and engineering. Scottish technology won world-wide acclaim: Kipling was not the only one to admire the Scottish engineer. The energy and enterprise showed on the Clyde from the beginning of the Industrial Revolution until the coming of the Great Depression after the First World War were remarkable. Was Scotland especially hit by depression when it came because Clydeside had put all its eggs into one basket (heavy industry) and was thus particularly vulnerable to an economic policy emanating from Westminster? And was it as a result of the Union that after the great railway merger of 1923 the control of Scot-land's railways went to London and the associated engineering works, that had been second only to shipbuilding among Glasgow's heavy industries, moved to England? If Edinburgh's development in the nineteenth century as the primly genteel professional city against whose morality the young Robert Louis Stevenson so fiercely rebelled, if Glasgow's problems of slums and squalor and Irish immigration and sectarian hatred and general violence co-existing with its energy and inventiveness made those two cities emblematic of some of the paradoxes of Scotland's urban culture in the second century after the Union, can we say that these things are the *result* of the Union? In a sense, historically, all *post hoc* must be *propter hoc*. What happens afterwards follows on what happens before. The problem in discussing, in however general a way, the long-term effects of the Union is to know how to weigh and where to place the innumerable factors that developed between 1707 and the present. But if we cannot satisfactorily answer the question, 'What has the Union done for Scotland?' perhaps we can, in a final chapter, give some examples, produce some reflections, and cite some recent instances, that might help in some degree to clarify the picture.

12. 'How can I be sad upon my wedding day?'

There is a tradition that on 1 May 1707, when the Union came into force, somebody managed to gain access to the bells of the High Kirk of St Giles in Edinburgh and rang on them the tune of the old song, 'How can I be sad upon my wedding day'. The tradition reflects an ambivalence of feeling about the Union that is found in Scotland again and again after 1707. This ambiguity is seen both in Burns and in Scott. In some moods Burns accepted the Union and expressed a British patriotism:

> Be Britain still to Britain true,
>   Amang oursels united;
> For never but by British hands
>   Must British wrangs be righted.

But he was also embued with a fiercely held Scottish patriotism, which expressed itself more frequently and more violently than his sense of loyalty to Britain. He re-wrote an old anti-Union song with passion:

> Fareweel to a' our Scottish fame,
>   Fareweel our ancient glory;
> Fareweel even to the Scotish name,
>   Sae fam'd in martial story!
> Now Sark rins o'er the Solway sands,
>   And Tweed rins to the ocean,
> To mark where England's province stands,
>   Such a parcel of rogues in a nation! . . .

O would, or I had seen the day
    That treason thus could sell us,
My auld grey head had lien in clay,
    Wi' Bruce and loyal Wallace!
But pith and power, till my last hour,
    I'll mak this declaration;
We're bought and sold for English gold.
    Such a parcel of rogues in a nation!

Scott, too, though he talked in *Tales of a Grandfather* of 'this happy union of England and Scotland' and made clear in *Waverley* and other novels that he thought the Union had made for progress and civilization, risked a breach with his good friends, the second Lord Melville, by publishing in 1826 his nationalistic *Letters of Malachi Malagrowther*. This work, though ostensibly on the limited question of the right of the Scottish banks to issue their own bank-notes (which the Government proposed to withdraw), breathed a spirit of fiery Scottish nationalism and fierce opposition to the 'disposition to change every thing in Scotland to an English model', with distinct overtones of a suggestion that if provoked too far Scotland's only recourse might be to secede from the Union.

We have already noted the attitude to the Scots language taken up by the *literati* of eighteenth-century Scotland: that too was symbolic of an uneasiness, a cultural ambiguity, which is also reflected in the growth of a special kind of Scottish urban gentility that sharply separated what might be called establishment culture from vernacular culture. Such problems and divisions of course existed also in England, but in Scotland they were of a special nature and sprang from genuine disorientation. Even in the Victorian years when so many Scots went out to govern the Empire or obtain prominent political or industrial positions in England there remained signs of this disorientation, either in nostalgia or in uncertainty about identity. With the loss of the Empire in our own time many nostalgic Scots came home and their children were more likely to turn to Scottish Nationalism than to British Imperialism to satisfy their national feelings.

Meanwhile, Britain was called 'England' everywhere except in Scotland, while Scotland was the name of a part-comic, part-romantic region of no defined political status or identity that was known for whisky, heather and tartan.

It took time for the Scottish people to realize the implications of their position. When Queen Victoria's son ascended the throne as Edward VII of Britain, there were few voices in Scotland to point out that he was Edward VII of England only, but the *first* Edward to rule over Britain. The assumption implied in the title Edward VII that the earlier Edwards had also been kings of all Britain was a deep insult to Scottish national feeling and completely ignored the clear implications of the Treaty of Union. When, half a century later, the present Queen ascended the throne as Queen Elizabeth II, there was a great outcry in Scotland against her assumption of that title with reference to Britain as a whole, for it assumed that Queen Elizabeth I had also been Queen of Scotland. This time most Scots were clearly aware of the issue. In Scotland the Queen was Queen Elizabeth I, or simply Queen Elizabeth (as England's first Elizabeth had been simply Queen Elizabeth) and ER rather than E II R should be inscribed on pillar boxes and other places requiring the royal cipher. Englishmen were totally at a loss to understand what all the fuss was about. It was, however, a Scottish Court that, in the case of *MacCormick and Another* v. *The Lord Advocate, 1953* refused John M. MacCormick's attempt to have the title 'Elizabeth II' made illegal in Scotland, though the Lord Advocate, Lord Cooper, 'hazarded the conjecture that an advisory opinion of the International Court of Justice might be competent'. In theory, Lord Cooper was wrong, for if the Union had abolished both England and Scotland as national entities to produce Great Britain, how could Scotland appeal against England when neither had a constitutional existence? At the same time Scotland *did* legally exist, for there was an established Church of Scotland, a Secretary of State for Scotland and other legal entities implying its existence.

The position, in fact, is full of paradoxes. If the Treaty of

Union was an international treaty between two sovereign states, it was concluded (as Professor T. B. Smith has argued) not by the two Parliaments, which did not exercise the prerogative of treaty-making powers, but by Anne in her capacity as Queen of Scotland with Anne in her capacity as Queen of England. As we have seen, the Treaty said nothing about the powers of the new Parliament of Great Britain that was to come into being at the Union, superseding the individual Parliaments of England and Scotland. But it was tacitly assumed that the new Parliament would inherit the powers of the old English rather than of the old Scottish Parliament, and no Act of the British Parliament has in fact ever been successfully challenged in the Scottish Courts. In other words, the Scots have implicitly accepted the English assumption that the Parliament of Great Britain inherited the powers of the Parliament of England and therefore its absolute omnipotence as a law-making power. On this view, Parliament could, if it wished, repeal any clause of the Treaty of Union. True, Lord Cooper, in the E II R case already referred to, argued that as the Scottish Parliament had not possessed the sovereignty claimed by the English Parliament it could not transmit this quality to the Parliament of Great Britain. But subsequent authorities have regarded this argument as purely academic, since (as James Kellas has put it in his book on the Scottish political system) 'the relationship between Scotland and England depends more on mutual accommodation and working the Act of Union in a proper spirit'. This is to say that the whole legal and constitutional basis of the Union remains in doubt, and it is worked pragmatically 'in a proper spirit'.

As we have seen, several Articles of the Union had already been nullified in the eighteenth and nineteenth centuries. By the end of the nineteenth century various administrative, electoral and judicial reforms had effectively abolished Articles XXI (guaranteeing the privileges of the royal burghs), XXII (on parliamentary elections) and XIX (on the organization of the law courts). Other minor economic and political arrangements were also reorganized in a way different from that laid down in the Treaty of

Union. The Articles remaining in force are essentially, I, II and III (dealing with the Union of the two kingdoms, the Protestant succession, and the Union of Parliaments), IV (freedom of trade and navigation), and others and parts of others dealing with uniformity of customs and excise, standardized coinage, the preservation of Scots law as a separate entity, representative peers, the abrogation of mutually hostile laws, and the establishment (though no longer all the exclusive rights) of the Church of Scotland (which was a separate Act forming part of the Treaty of Union).

Not many Scotsmen have been concerned with the niceties of legal and constitutional theory in expressing nationalist views. As Scottish parliamentary representation increased with parliamentary reform in the nineteenth century—especially with the third Reform Act of 1884—the place of the Westminister Parliament in British life as a whole seemed to become more secure. And with the establishment in 1885 of a Scottish Office headed by a Secretary for Scotland who soon gained a permanent place in the Cabinet, and the setting up in 1894 of a Scottish Grand Committee to look after purely Scottish Bills in the House and see that they were given adequate time, it might seem that Scottish content with the existing parliamentary system was guaranteed. In 1926 the Secretary for Scotland was elevated to the rank of Principal Secretary of State; in 1937 the Gilmour Committee, reporting on Scottish Administration, recommended that there should be a Scottish Office in Edinburgh and that the Secretary of State for Scotland should exercise a closer control of Scottish administration, and in 1939 St Andrew's House was opened in Edinburgh in response to this recommendation. These and other administrative reforms that have taken place from 1939 to the present day might have been expected to lessen Scottish feelings of national frustration. In fact, it is precisely during the period of these reforms that the modern Scottish national movement has developed.

The agitation for Irish Home Rule had some effect in Scotland in the early 1880s, when talk about Home Rule for Scotland became fairly common. In 1886 the Scottish Home Rule Association was formed, with the Member of Parliament for Caithness as its President and among its committee members R. B. Cunninghame-Graham, former Provosts of Glasgow and Paisley, a number of lawyers and ministers and a dozen Scottish Members of Parliament. These M.P.'s raised the matter of Home Rule for Scotland in the House of Commons in 1889, and brought the matter to a vote, with 79 out of 279 M.P.'s present voting for Home Rule, the Scots vote being 19 for and 22 against. In February 1890 the President of the Home Rule Association moved an amendment to the Address in reply to the Queen's Speech complaining that 'the present mode of legislating for the domestic affairs of Scotland is unsatisfactory' and stating that it was 'desirable, while retaining the supremacy of the Imperial Parliament, to devolve upon a Legislature in Scotland the consideration of the domestic affairs of the country'. The amendment was of course rejected, the Lord Advocate himself strongly opposing it on the ground that Scotland had been 'withdrawn from darkness' by the Union, which had provided nothing but splendid benefits to that country. Gladstone fiercely castigated the mover of the amendment, in spite of the fact that he conceded 'that the period between the Act of Union and the Reform Act of 1832 is not a very laudable or very creditable period in the history of Scottish Parliamentary representation'. Further motions for Home Rule within a federal system were brought forward unsuccessfully in the 1890s.

In 1908, fourteen years after the setting up of the Scottish Grand Committee, a Bill for Scottish Home Rule was introduced into the House of Commons by D. V. Pirrie and passed its first reading by 107 votes in a House of 359. This time the Scots members voted 41 in favour and nine against. But it got no further. A similar Bill was brought forward by Sir Hugh Dalziel in 1911 and passed its first reading, but again nothing more was done. This happened twice more during the next year, and in 1913 a Scottish Home Rule Bill got as far as a second reading. Between 1889 and 1914 the subject of Scottish Home Rule was before the House of Commons thirteen times. Then the outbreak of war stopped further discussion of the matter.

Scottish nationalism emerged again after the First World War in a somewhat different form. The Scottish Nationalist Party was formed in 1928 and a more cautious devolutionary party called the Scottish Party was founded in 1932: in 1934 the two amalgamated as the Scottish National Party. The emphasis was for a time more economic than organizational. With Scotland suffering so heavily during the Depression it was argued that the English connection was responsible and that Scotland was paying more to and receiving less from the Exchequer than was fair and just. In answer to this it was maintained that the precise contrary was true and that one consequence of the Depression's having hit Scotland so hard was that she was contributing less and receiving more. The argument about the net financial gain or loss to Scotland of her union with England has gone on continuously since then. The fact seems to be that the financial and economic affairs of Scotland and England are so intertwined that an accurate costing of the share of each (received or contributed) is impossible.

But the cultural argument was raised at least as urgently as the economic argument in the period between the two world wars. The Scottish Renaissance associated with the name of Hugh MacDiarmid (C. M. Grieve) was concerned with the integrity of Scottish culture; with the revival of an authentic Scottish language both Lowland Scots and Gaelic; with the condemnation of English and Anglo-American influences on Scottish ways of life and thought; with the rediscovery of a genuine national identity for Scotland. In MacDiarmid's case (though his was a special instance, as he was both a Nationalist and a Communist) Scottish nationalism was associated with a pan-Celticism and a belief in the importance of reviving a Celtic alliance of Scots, Welshmen, Cornishmen and Irish against Anglo-Saxondom. (This view enjoyed a brief revival in the early years of the Second World War in the movement known as The New Alliance, the alliance being essentially Scots-Irish.) During the inter-war period Scottish Nationalism was on the whole a matter of cultural and ideological debate rather than of economic strategy. The growth of 'Red Clydeside' and the emergence of a depressed industrial

Scotland as a dependable source of support for the Left in British politics, in opposition both to the urban genteel tradition we have already discussed and to the deferential attitude prevalent in so many of the country areas, was much more significant in terms of practical politics. It is the Scottish Labour vote that has brought the Labour party to power in its periods of success, and without the built-in Labour majority in Scotland that developed out of the left-wing activities of Clydeside in the 1920s and the Depression years of the early 1930s Labour would not have gained power. It is precisely that Labour majority in Scotland that is threatened today by the successes of the Scottish National Party in traditional Labour constituencies.

A mass of periodicals—many of them 'little magazines', most of them short-lived—testify to the cultural argument about Scottish identity during and after the Second World War. *The New Alliance* (turning into *The New Alliance and Scots Review*), *Poetry Scotland*, *Scottish Periodical*, *Lines Review*, *The Saltire Review*, *The New Saltire*, *The Voice of Scotland*, *Scottish International*, among many others, reflect a wide political spectrum while sharing a concern about the nature and quality of Scottish culture. This concern had not lapsed during the war, when in spite of (or because of) a coalition government and an electoral truce between the major political parties a sharp debate between activist and moderate Nationalists led to a period of internal conflict which lasted well into the 1950s. In spite of this the Nationalists gained votes in by-elections and at a by-election in April 1945 Dr Robert McIntyre won Motherwell for the Nationalists, but the seat reverted to Labour at the General Election three months later.

After the war the divisions among nationalists were reflected in a variety of activities. In 1947–8 a Scottish Convention campaigned for a Scottish Parliament, finding support among considerable numbers of professional people. In 1948 a Government White Paper curtly rejected the demand for an inquiry into the case for devolution. In 1949 John MacCormick founded the Scottish Covenant, a campaign to collect signatures in support of a

Scottish Parliament within the framework of the United Kingdom, and got nearly two million. The Covenant movement ebbed away in the mid-1950s but it left behind a growing consciousness of the claims of Scotland to some kind of devolution. Nationalist feeling grew rapidly in the late 1960s and in the 1970s and was reflected in renewed and strengthened support to the Scottish National Party, until now there are eleven members of the Party in Parliament. The discovery of oil in the North Sea and the piping of it ashore to Scotland encouraged the Scottish National Party to claim that it was 'Scotland's oil' and to envisage a rosy economic future for an independent Scotland sustained by its oil revenues and perhaps giving a helping hand to an impoverished England.

That the present popularity of the Scottish National Party reflects a genuine feeling among large numbers of Scots that their country requires some kind of devolution seems clear. In many respects nationalist feeling is a generalized cultural feeling rather than a specific desire for a particular political move, and certainly there is a considerable range of political colour among members of the Party. The argument about oil, so vociferously raised, applies at best only to the short term, since the quantity of oil is not limitless and Scotland will have to come to terms with its economy after the oil is exhausted (in, say, forty years?). Further, the oil argument deflects attention from the real question, which concerns Scotland's national and cultural identity. If Scots who originally voted for the Union did so on economic grounds, those who came to object to it in a later age have mostly been concerned with the cultural argument. Those who despair about the organization of the Scottish economy are still more likely to support the left wing of the Labour Party than the Nationalists (although the emergence of a Scottish Labour Party as a specifically left-wing nationalist party may deflect some from this course). The unease that leads people in Scotland to associate themselves with Scottish nationalism is basically a cultural unease, a concern for the Scottish quality of Scottish life, an anxiety about Scottish identity. It is also a kind of hurt pride.

It is perhaps strange that so long after the Treaty of Union the hurt to Scottish pride is showing itself so vividly. But it is there, and it will not be healed until something is done about it. Precisely what should be done is the great subject for debate in Scotland today.

Select Bibliography

Barrow, G. W. S., *Robert Bruce and the Community of the Realm of Scotland*, London, 1965.

[Boyer, Abel] *The History of the Reign of Queen Anne, Digested into Annals*, London, 1705.

Brown, P. Hume (Ed.), *Letters Relating to Scotland in the Reign of Queen Anne by James Ogilvy, First Earl of Seafield, and Others*, Edinburgh, 1915.

Burnet, Gilbert, *Bishop Burnet's History of His Own Time*, 3 vols., London, 1725.

Burton, J. H., *The History of Scotland*, Vol. VIII, Edinburgh and London, 1898.

Correspondence of George Baillie of Jerviswood 1702–1708, Edinburgh, 1842.

Craig, Sir Thomas, *Scotland's Soveraignty Asserted*, trans. George Ridpath, Edinburgh 1695.

Craig, Sir Thomas, *De Unione Regnorum Britanniae*, ed. C. S. Terry, Edinburgh, 1909.

Daiches, David, *The Paradox of Scottish Culture*, London, 1964.

Defoe, Daniel, *Defoe's Review, Reproduced from the Original Editions with an Introduction and Bibliographical Notes* by A. W. Secord, New York, 1965.

Defoe, Daniel, *The History of the Union of Great Britain*, Edinburgh, 1709.

Defoe, Daniel, *The Letters of Daniel Defoe*, ed. G. H. Healey, Oxford, 1955.

Donaldson, Gordon, *Scottish Historical Documents*, Edinburgh, 1974.

Duncan, A. A. M., *Scotland, The Making of the Kingdom*, Edinburgh and London, 1975.

Ferguson, William, *Scotland 1689 to the Present*, Edinburgh and London, 1968.

[Fletcher, Andrew, of Saltoun] *Speeches by a Member of the Parliament which began at Edinburgh the 6th May 1703*, Edinburgh, 1703.

Fletcher, Andrew, of Saltoun, *The Political Works of Andrew Fletcher, Esq. of Saltoun*, Glasgow, 1749.

Gray, J. M. (Ed.), *Memoirs of the Life of Sir John Clerk of Penicuik, 1676–1755*, Edinburgh, 1892.

Hamilton, Henry, *An Economic History of Scotland in the Eighteenth Century*, Oxford, 1963.

Hanham, J. H., *Scottish Nationalism*, London, 1969.

Henderson, Isabel, *The Picts*, London, 1967.

Hume, Sir David, of Crossrig, *A Diary of the Proceedings in the Parliament and Privy Council of Scotland. May 21, MDCC–March 7, MDCC VII*, Edinburgh, 1828.

Kellas, James G., *The Scottish Political System*, Cambridge, 1973.

[Lockhart, George, of Carnwath], *Memoirs Concerning the Affairs of Scotland from Queen Anne's Accession to the Commencement of the Union*, London, 1714.

Lockhart, George, of Carnwath, *The Lockhart Papers*, 2 vols., London, 1817.

McIlwain, C. H. (Ed.), *Political Works of James I*, London, 1918.

Mackenzie, W. C., *Andrew Fletcher of Saltoun, His Life and Times*, Edinburgh, 1935.

Mackinnon, James, *The Union of England and Scotland*, London, 1896.

McLaren, Moray, *If Freedom Fail*, London, 1964.

Mathieson, W. L., *Scotland and the Union*, Glasgow, 1905.

Menzies, Gordon (Ed.), *Who are the Scots?*, London, 1971.

Minutes of the Proceedings in Parliament, Edinburgh, 1693–1707.

Mitchison, Rosalind, *A History of Scotland*, London, 1970.

Nicholson, R. G., *Scotland, The Later Middle Ages*, Edinburgh and London, 1976.

Nobbs, Douglas, *England and Scotland 1603–1707*, London, 1952.

Phillipson, N. T. and Mitchison, Rosalind (Ed.), *Scotland in the Age of Improvement*, Edinburgh, 1970.

Pryde, G. S., *The Treaty of Union of Scotland and England 1707*, London and Edinburgh, 1950.

Rae, T. I. (Ed.), *The Union of 1707: Its Impact on Scotland*, Glasgow, 1974.

Rait, R. S., *The Parliaments of Scotland*, Glasgow, 1924.

Ridpath, George, *A Discourse upon the Union of Scotland and England*, n.p. 1702.

[Ridpath, George, Compiler], *The Proceedings of the Parliament of Scotland Begun at Edinburgh 6th May 1703*, Edinburgh, 1704.

Ritchie, R. K. G., *The Normans in Scotland*, Edinburgh, 1954.

Smith, T. B., *British Justice, the Scottish Contribution*, London, 1961.

Smout, T. C., *A History of the Scottish People, 1560–1830*, London, 1969.

Smout, T. C., *Scottish Trade on the Eve of the Union*, Edinburgh, 1963.

Smout, T. C., 'The Road to Union' in Homes, Geoffrey (Ed.), *Britain after the Glorious Revolution*, London, 1969.

Smout, T. C. (Ed.), 'Sir John Clerk's Observations on the Present Circumstances of Scotland, 1730' in *Miscellany of the Scottish History Society, Volume X*, Edinburgh, 1965.

Tarbat, George, Viscount, and others (Collectors and Compilers), *The Laws and Acts made in ... Parliament, Collected and Extracted from the Registers and Records of Parliament*, Edinburgh, 1731.

Wilson, D. H., *James VI and I*, London, 1956.

Index

Index